STUDY GUIDE

Henry Borne
S. Mikael Jansson

SOCIETY
The Basics

Second Canadian Edition

John J. Macionis
S. Mikael Jansson
Cecilia Benoit

Toronto

© 2002 Pearson Education Canada Inc., Toronto, Ontario

All rights reserved. This publication is protected by copyright, and permission should be obtained from the publisher prior to any prohibited reproduction, storage in a retrieval system, or transmission in any form or by any means, electronic, mechanical, photocopying, recording, or likewise. For information regarding permission, write to the Permissions Department.

ISBN 0-13-061297-9

Acquisitions Editor: Jessica Mosher
Developmental Editor: Dawn du Quesnay
Production Editor: Sherry Torchinsky
Production Coordinator: Peggy Brown

1 2 3 4 5   05 04 03 02 01

Printed and bound in Canada.

Contents

Preface	v
Chapter 1: Sociology: Perspective, Theory, and Method	1
Chapter 2: Culture	21
Chapter 3: Socialization: From Infancy to Old Age	39
Chapter 4: Social Interaction In Everyday Life	55
Chapter 5: Groups and Organizations	69
Chapter 6: Deviance	85
Chapter 7: Sexuality	103
Chapter 8: Social Stratification	117
Chapter 9: Global Stratification	139
Chapter 10: Gender Stratification	153
Chapter 11: Race and Ethnicity	169
Chapter 12: Economics and Politics	185
Chapter 13: Family and Religion	215
Chapter 14: Education and Health	243
Chapter 15: Population, Urbanization, and Environment	269
Chapter 16: Social Change: Modern and Postmodern Societies	291

Preface

We welcome you to the world of sociology and hope that this introductory course will entice you to join our quest to understand human social activity. This Study Guide offers many different strategies to help you study the sociological ideas and issues presented in **Society: The Basics, Second Canadian Edition**. We all have different methods of learning and we encourage you to experiment to find the strategy that works for you.

Effective learners are those that become actively involved in the learning process. Initially, the best way to do this is to read with a marker and pencil in your hand. Use the marker to highlight the most important parts of each section of your text book, and use the pencil to write notes to yourself about questions, comments or reservations you have about the material. When you feel confident that you have absorbed the material in the text book, turn to this study guide to help you review and think about the material you have already studied.

The Study Guide has been organized into several sections to accompany each chapter in the text. A **Chapter Outline** provides the basis for organizing segments of information in each chapter of the text. The **Learning Objectives** identify the material you should focus on while reviewing and studying each chapter in the text. A section entitled **Key Concepts** lists the important concepts from each chapter. Next, the section called **Important Researchers** lists the researchers cited in the text and provides a space for you to write significant ideas, research findings, accomplishments, etc., for each researcher. The **Study Questions** section includes true-false, multiple-choice, matching, fill-in-the-blank, definition and short-answer questions. These questions are followed by a section with the **Answers to Study Questions**, which also list page references in the text where the answer is given in more detail. The final section, **Analysis and Comment**, provides space for you to raise questions and make comments on the many boxes presented in the text.

Sociological knowledge helps us understand the world around us. Become an active participant in your society and use your knowledge every day.

Sociology: Perspective, Theory, and Method

PART I: CHAPTER OUTLINE

1. The Sociological Perspective
    A. Seeing the General in the Particular
    B. Seeing the Strange in the Familiar
    C. Seeing Individuality in Social Context
    D. Benefits of the Sociological Perspective
    E. Applied Sociology
    F. The Importance of Global Perspective
2. The Origins of Sociology
    A. Science and Sociology
    B. Social Change and Sociology
    C. Marginal Voices
3. Sociological Theory
    A. The Structural-Functional Paradigm
    B. The Social-Conflict Paradigm
    C. The Symbolic-Interaction Paradigm
4. Scientific Sociology
    A. Concepts, Variables, and Measurement
    B. Correlation and Cause
    C. The Ideal of Objectivity
    D. A Second Framework: Interpretive Sociology
    E. A Third Framework: Critical Sociology
    F. Research and Gender
    G. Research Ethics
5. Research Methods
    A. Testing a Hypothesis: The Experiment
    B. Asking Questions: The Survey
    C. In the Field: Participant Observation
    D. The Second Time Around: Existing Sources
    E. Putting It All Together: Ten Steps in Sociological Research
6. Summary
7. Key Concepts
8. Critical-Thinking Questions
9. Applications and Exercises
10. Sites to See

PART II: LEARNING OBJECTIVES

1. To be able to define sociology and understand the basic components of the sociological perspective.
2. To be able to provide examples of the ways in which social forces affect our everyday lives.
3. To recognize the importance of taking a global perspective in order to recognize the interdependence of our world's nations and people.
4. To be able to recognize the benefits of using the sociological perspective.
5. To be able to identify important historical factors in the development of the discipline of sociology as a science.
6. To be able to identify and discuss the differences between the three major theoretical paradigms used by sociologists in the analysis of society.
7. To understand the difference between sociology as a science and common sense.
8. To become familiar with the basic elements of science and how they are used in sociological investigation.
9. To develop an understanding about the difference between correlation and cause.
10. To recognize the difficulties in maintaining objectivity in sociological research.
11. To be able to distinguish between *scientific, interpretive,* and *critical* sociological frameworks.
12. To recognize how research is affected by *gender*.
13. To begin to view ethical considerations involved in studying people.
14. To become familiar with research methods used by sociologists in the investigation of society.
15. To be able to identify and describe each of the ten steps in sociological research.

PART III: KEY CONCEPTS

Define each of the following concepts in the space provided or on a separate paper. Check the accuracy of your answers by referring to the key concepts section at the end of the chapter in the text as well as referring to italicized definitions located throughout the chapter. Do the same for each chapter as you read through the text during the semester.

Perspective and Theory

global perspective

high-income countries

latent functions

low-income countries

macro-level orientation

manifest functions

micro-level orientation

middle-income countries

positivism

social-conflict paradigm

social dysfunction

social function

social structure

sociology

stereotype

structural-functional paradigm

symbolic-interaction paradigm

theoretical paradigm

theory

Methods
cause and effect

concept

correlation

critical sociology

experiment

gender

interpretive sociology

measurement

participant observation

reliability

Society: The Basics, Second Canadian Edition

research method

science

survey

validity

variable

PART IV: IMPORTANT RESEARCHERS
Write down the important points made by each of these researchers:

Emile Durkheim   Harriet Martineau

Karl Marx   Nellie McClung

Max Weber   W.E.B. Du Bois

Robert Merton   Auguste Comte

Peter Berger   C. Wright Mills

PART V: STUDY QUESTIONS
True-False

1. T F A major component of the sociological perspective is the attempt to seek the *particular in the general*.
2. T F Emile Durkheim's research on *suicide* illustrates the point that not all aspects of social life can be meaningfully studied using the sociological perspective.
3. T F Protestants and Catholics, men and women, the married and unmarried have different suicide rates. Emile Durkheim explained these differences in terms of *social integration*.
4. T F Females have *higher suicide rates* than males.
5. T F The *middle-income countries* of the world are primarily found in Latin America, Eastern Europe, and the former Soviet Union.
6. T F The discipline of *sociology* first emerged in Europe during the nineteenth century.
7. T F *Positivism* is an approach to understanding the world based on science.
8. T F Auguste Comte saw sociology as the product of a three-stage historical development, including the *theological stage*, the *metaphysical stage*, and the *scientific stage*.
9. T F Nellie McClung was instrumental in changing changes that led to Canadian women being included in the definition of *person* under the *British North American Act*.
10. T F A *theory* is a statement of how and why specific facts are related.
11. T F *Latent functions* refer to social processes which appear on the surface to be functional for society, but which are actually detrimental.
12. T F The *symbolic-interaction* and *social-conflict* paradigms both operate from a *micro-level orientation*.
13. T F The *symbolic-interactionist paradigm* presents society less in terms of abstract generalizations and more as everyday experiences.
14. T F The core question of the *structural-functional paradigm* is: How is society divided?
15. T F Our authors argues that a major strength of sociology is that it is basically just using *common sense*.
16. T F *Science* is defined as a logical system that bases knowledge on direct, systematic observation.
17. T F A *concept* is defined as the process of determining the value of a variable in a specific case.
18. T F The *mode* is the statistical term referring to the value which occurs most often in a series of numbers.
19. T F *Reliability* refers to consistency in measurement.
20. T F If two variables are *correlated*, by definition one is an *independent variable* and one is a *dependent variable*.

21. T F Max Weber argued that people involved in scientific research must strive to be *value-free*.
22. T F *Interpretation* is rarely beneficial in sociological investigation.
23. T F *Critical sociology* is the study of society that focuses on the need for social change.
24. T F *Interpretive sociology* is directly linked to the structural-functional paradigm.
25. T F *Androcentricity* refers to approaching an issue from a male perspective.
26. T F A *sample* refers to a research method in which subjects respond to a series of items in a questionnaire or interview.
27. T F The first step in the scientific research process should always be to determine what *research design* will be used to obtain data.
28. T F A *generalization* is defined as an exaggerated description that one applies to all people in some category.

Multiple Choice

1. The *GAP* discussed in your textbook is
   a) Government Assistance to the Poor.
   b) an all-girl school in Victoria, BC.
   c) a location in Regina where sociologists meet to talk about social issues.
   d) a residence hall at Athabasca University.

2. What is the *essential wisdom* of sociology?
   a) Patterns in life are predestined.
   b) Society is essentially non-patterned.
   c) Surrounding society affects our actions, thoughts, and feelings.
   d) Common sense needs to guide sociological investigations.

3. The sociological perspective involves *seeing the strange in the familiar*. Which of the following best provides the essential meaning of this phrase?
   a) Sociology interprets social life primarily relying on common sense.
   b) Sociologists believe intuition rather than logic is the preferred way to study society.
   c) Sociologists focus on the bizarre behaviours that occur in society.
   d) Sociologists work to avoid the assumption that human behaviour is simply a matter of what people decide to do.

4. Which sociologist linked the incidence of *suicide* to the degree of *social integration* of different categories of people?
   a) Emile Durkheim
   b) Max Weber
   c) Robert Merton
   d) C. Wright Mills
   e) Karl Marx

5. Which of the following is/are identified as situations that stimulate *sociological thinking*?
   a) social diversity
   b) social marginality
   c) social crisis
   d) all of the above
   e) none of the above

6. In that sociology has an impact on some public policy and also helps prepare people for the many different types of jobs illustrates the _____ nature of this field of study.
   a) micro
   b) applied
   c) theoretical
   d) secondary

7. _____ refers to the study of the larger world and our society's place in it.
   a) Interpretive sociology
   b) Critical sociology
   c) Global perspective
   d) Holistic analysis

8. *Low-income countries* are described in the text as
   a) nations with little industrialization in which most people are poor.
   b) nations with limited natural resources and large populations.
   c) nations with a per capita income of less than $20,000.
   d) nations with no industrialization and limited natural resources.

9. Which of the following is *not* identified by the author as a reason a *global perspective* is so important?
   a) Societies the world over are increasingly interconnected.
   b) Many problems that we face in Canada are not found in other societies.
   c) Thinking globally is a good way to learn more about ourselves.
   d) All of the above are identified by the authors as reasons why a global perspective is so important.

10. The term *sociology* was coined in 1838 by
    a) Auguste Comte.
    b) Karl Marx.
    c) Herbert Spencer.
    d) Emile Durkheim.
    e) Max Weber.

11. According to Auguste Comte, the key to understanding society was to look at it
    a) using common sense.
    b) using intuition.
    c) theologically.
    d) metaphysically.
    e) scientifically.

12. *Positivism* is the idea that _____, rather than any other type of human understanding, is the path to knowledge.
    a) human nature
    b) science
    c) faith
    d) optimism
    e) common sense

13. Two *founders of sociology* who had radically different views on society—one more traditional and conservative, the other more critical and focussed on change—were:
    a) C. Wright Mills and Robert Merton.
    b) Nellie McClung and Harriet Martineau.
    c) Emile Durkheim and Robert Merton.
    d) Auguste Comte and Karl Marx.
    e) Karl Marx and C. Wright Mills.

14. _____ translated the works of Auguste Comte from French to English in 1853. She also was a noted scholar in her own right, revealing the evils of slavery and arguing for laws to protect factory workers.
    a) Jane Addams
    b) Lois Benjamin
    c) Ruth Bogda
    d) Irene Rappoport
    e) Harriet Martineau

15. A basic image of society that guides thinking and research is the definition for
    a) a theoretical paradigm.
    b) manifest functions.
    c) social marginality.
    d) positivism.

16. Any relatively stable pattern of social behaviour refers to
    a) social functions.
    b) theories.
    c) social structure.
    d) positivism.

17. Consequences of social structure which are largely *unrecognized* and *unintended* are called
    a) paradigms.
    b) manifest functions.
    c) latent functions.
    d) social integration.
    e) social marginality.

18. Sometimes social structures can have undesirable consequences for the operation of society. Robert Merton called these
    a) paradigms.
    b) social dysfunctions.
    c) latent functions.
    d) social integration.

19. Which of the following is a criticism of *structural-functionalism*?
    a) This theoretical paradigm focuses too much attention on social conflict.
    b) This theoretical paradigm attends to questions concerning how life is experienced by individuals on a day-to-day basis while ignoring larger social structures.
    c) This theoretical paradigm tends to ignore inequalities which can generate tension and conflict.
    d) This theoretical paradigm stresses the functional value of social change, while ignoring the integrative qualities of different social institutions.

20. Which of the following theoretical perspectives is best suited for analysis using a *macro-level* orientation?
    a) dramaturgical analysis
    b) social exchange theory
    c) symbolic-interactionist paradigm
    d) ethnomethodology
    e) social-conflict paradigm

21. The questions "How is society experienced?" and, "How do individuals attempt to shape the reality perceived by others?" are most likely asked by a researcher using which of the following theoretical paradigms?
    a) structural-functional
    b) symbolic-interaction
    c) social Darwinism
    d) social-conflict
    e) none of the above

22. _____ *evidence* is information we can verify with our senses.
    a) Consensual
    b) Common sense
    c) Intrapsychic
    d) Holistic
    e) Empirical

23. _____ is a logical system that bases knowledge on direct, systematic observation.
    a) Research method
    b) Sociological investigation
    c) Hypothesis
    d) Science
    e) Theory

24. Which of the following common sense statements is *false* according to empirical evidence?
    a) Differences in social behaviour of women and men reflect "human nature."
    b) Canada is a middle-class society where most people are more or less equal.
    c) People marry because they are in love.
    d) All of the above.
    e) None of the above.

25. A _____ is a mental construct that represents some part of the world, inevitably in a simplified form.
    a) variable
    b) concept
    c) hypothesis
    d) research design
    e) measurement

26. Specifying exactly what is to be measured in assigning a value to a variable is called
    a) validity.
    b) objectivity.
    c) operationalizing a variable.
    d) reliability.
    e) control.

27. The *arithmetic average* in a series of numbers is the
    a) control.
    b) median.
    c) mode.
    d) mean.
    e) conceptualization.

28. The *descriptive statistic* that represents the value that occurs *midway* in a series of numbers is called the
    a) median.
    b) correlation.
    c) mode.
    d) norm.
    e) mean.

29. The quality of *consistency* in measurement is known as
    a) spuriousness.
    b) reliability.
    c) empirical evidence.
    d) objectivity.
    e) validity.

30. Measuring what one *intends* to measure is the quality of measurement known as
    a) reliability.
    b) operationalization.
    c) validity.
    d) control.
    e) objectivity.

31. A higher level of education causes greater earnings over one's lifetime. In this case, *higher level of education* is
    a) a spurious variable.
    b) a dependent variable.
    c) an independent variable.
    d) the median.
    e) the control variable.

32. An apparent, although false, relationship between two (or more) variables caused by some other variable refers to
   a) a deductive correlation.
   b) an inductive correlation.
   c) a replicated correlation.
   d) an operational correlation.
   e) a spurious correlation.

33. A state of personal neutrality in conducting research is known as
   a) subjective interpretation.
   b) objectivity.
   c) control variable.
   d) spurious relationship.
   e) validity.

34. According to Max Weber, it is essential that researchers be _____ in their investigations.
   a) value-free
   b) subjective
   c) spurious
   d) selective in their reporting of facts
   e) concerned about social welfare

35. The study of society that focuses on the meanings people attach to their social world refers to
   a) critical sociology.
   b) quantitative sociology.
   c) residual sociology.
   d) interpretive sociology.

36. _____ is the study of society focussing on the need for social change.
   a) Androcentricity
   b) Qualitative research
   c) Critical sociology
   d) Interpretive sociology

37. The issue of *androcentricity* relates to
   a) overgeneralization.
   b) social activism.
   c) economic elitism.
   d) gender bias.
   e) political correctness.

38. A systematic plan for conducting research is the definition for
   a) theory.
   b) hypothesis.
   c) operationalizing a variable.
   d) sample.
   e) research method.

39. Which *research method* is explanatory and is usually used to test hypotheses?
   a) the survey
   b) participant observation
   c) the experiment
   d) the use of existing sources
   e) the interview

40. Sociology is not involved in *stereotyping* because
   a) sociologists do not indiscriminately apply any generalization to all individuals.
   b) sociologists base their generalizations on research.
   c) sociologists strive to be fair-minded.
   d) All of the above.
   e) None of the above.

Matching

Perspective and Theory

1. ____ The study of the larger world and our society's place in it.
2. ____ Nations with limited industrialization and moderate personal income.
3. ____ Saw sociology as a product of a three-stage historical development.
4. ____ A way of understanding based on science.
5. ____ A statement of how and why specific facts are related.
6. ____ A framework for building theory based on the assumption that society is a complex system whose parts work together to promote solidarity and stability.
7. ____ Relatively stable patterns of social behaviour.
8. ____ The largely unrecognized and unintended consequences of social structure.
9. ____ A framework for building theory that sees society as an arena of inequality that generates conflict and change.
10. ____ A close-up focus on social interactions in specific situations.

a. common sense
b. theory
c. social-conflict paradigm
d. Third-World nations
e. Herbert Spencer
f. sociological imagination
g. middle-income countries
h. latent functions
i. global perspective
j. social structure
k. Auguste Comte
l. positivism
m. structural-functional paradigm
n. macro-level orientation
o. sociology
p. micro-level orientation

Methods

1. ____ A logical system that bases knowledge on direct, systematic observation.
2. ____ A mental construct that represents an aspect of the world, inevitably in a somewhat simplified way.
3. ____ The quality of measurement gained by measuring precisely what one intends to measure.

4. ____ A relationship in which two (or more) variables change together.
5. ____ An apparent, although false, relationship between two (or more) variables caused by some other variable.
6. ____ A state of personal neutrality in conducting research.
7. ____ A research method in which subjects respond to a series of statements and questions in a questionnaire of interview.
8. ____ A part of a population that represents the whole.
9. ____ Fieldwork by cultural anthropologists is an example of this type of research.
10. ____ A research method in which a researcher uses data collected by others.

a. survey
b. objectivity
c. participant observation
d. concept
e. sample
f. existing sources
g. correlation
h. validity
i. spurious
j. science

Fill-in-the-blank

1. The systematic study of human society is the definition for _____.

2. Emile Durkheim reasoned that the variation in *suicide rates* between different categories of people had to do with *social* _____.

3. A _____ _____ is the study of the larger world and our society's place in it.

4. Canada, the United States, and most of the nations of Western Europe are classified in terms of economic development as being _____-income *countries*.

5. Three important reasons for taking a *global perspective* include: societies around the world are increasingly _____, many human problems that we face in Canada are far more _____ elsewhere, and it is a good way to learn more about _____.

6. The development of sociology as an academic discipline was shaped within the context of three revolutionary changes in Europe during the seventeenth and eighteenth centuries. These included *a new* _____ _____, the *growth of* _____, and _____ *change*.

7. Auguste Comte asserted that scientific sociology was a result of a progression throughout history of thought and understanding in *three stages*: the _____, _____, and _____.

8. A _____ is a statement of how and why specific facts are related.

9. A _____ _____ provides a basic image of society that guides thinking and research.

10. Concern with small-scale patterns of social interaction, such as *symbolic-interaction theory*, operates through a _____-_____ orientation.

11. _____ *evidence* refers to information we can verify with our senses.

12. _____ is a procedure for determining the value of a variable in a specific case.

13. _____ refers to two variables that *vary together,* such as number of years of education and earned income.

14. The state of *personal neutrality* in conducting research is referred to as _____.

15. The German sociologist _____ distinguished between *value-relevant* choice of research and *value-free* conduct of scientific investigation.

16. _____ *sociology* is the study of society that focuses on the meanings people attach to their social world.

17. _____ *sociology* is the study of society that focuses on the need for social change.

18. Five ways in which *gender* can jeopardize good research include: _____, _____, _____, gender _____, _____ standards, and _____.

19. The _____ is a *research model* in which subjects respond to a series of statements or questions in a *questionnaire* or an *interview*.

20. A _____ is a part of a population that represents the whole.

21. Two types of surveys include _____ and _____.

22. A _____ is an exaggerated description applied to all people in some category.

Definition and Short-Answer

1. Differentiate between the concepts *manifest* and *latent functions* and provide an illustration for each.
2. Discuss Emile Durkheim's explanation of how *suicide rates* vary between different categories of people. Explain how this research demonstrates the application of the *sociological perspective*.
3. What are the three types of countries identified in the text as measured by their level of *economic development*? What are the characteristics of the countries that represent each of the three types?
4. What are the three major reasons why a *global perspective* is so important today?
5. What were three *social changes* in seventeenth and eighteenth century Europe that provided the context for the development of *sociology* as a scientific discipline?
6. What are the three major components of the *sociological perspective*? Describe and provide an illustration for each.
7. What are the three major *theoretical paradigms* used by sociologists? Identify two key questions raised by each in the analysis of society. Identify one weakness for each of these paradigms for understanding the nature of human social life.
8. How do the three theoretical paradigms help us understand the place of *spots* in our society?
9. What are three reasons why sociology is *not to be considered* nothing more than *stereotyping*?
10. What are four *benefits* of using the sociological perspective?
11. What is the relationship between *sociology* and *social marginality*? Provide an illustration.
12. What are the three factors which must be determined to conclude that a *cause and effect* relationship between two variables may exist?
13. Margrit Eichler points out five dangers to sound research that involves *gender*. Identify and define each.
14. Define the concept *hypothesis*. Further, write your own hypothesis and operationalize the variables identified.
15. Identify two advantages and two disadvantages for each of the four major *research methods* used by sociologists.
16. What are the basic steps of the sociological *research process*? Briefly describe each.

17. Three illustrations are provided to show that *common sense* does not always guide us to a meaningful sense of reality. What two examples can you give concerning common sense not paving the way toward our understanding of what is really happening in social life?
18. Identify and define the *major elements* of scientific investigation.
19. Using standardized high school exams as an example, illustrate the difference between *reliability* and *validity*.
20. What are the basic guidelines for *research ethics* in sociological research?

PART VI: ANSWERS TO STUDY QUESTIONS

True-False

1. F (p. 4)	8. T (p. 10)	15. F (p. 14)	22. F (p. 19)
2. F (p. 5)	9. T (p. 12)	16. T (p. 14)	23. T (p. 19)
3. T (p. 5)	10. T (p. 12)	17. F (p. 15)	24. F (p. 19)
4. F (p. 5)	11. F (p. 13)	18. T (p. 15)	25. T (p. 20)
5. T (pp. 8-9)	12. F (p. 14)	19. T (p. 15)	26. F (p. 22)
6. T (p. 10)	13. T (p. 14)	20. F (p. 15)	27. F (p. 23)
7. T (p. 10)	14. F (p. 15)	21. T (p. 18)	28. F (p. 24)

Multiple Choice

1. b (p. 3)	11. e (p. 10)	21. b (p. 15)	31. c (p. 18)
2. c (p. 3)	12. b (p. 10)	22. e (p. 15)	32. e (p. 18)
3. d (p. 4)	13. d (p. 11)	23. d (p. 15)	33. b (p. 18)
4. a (p. 5)	14. e (p. 12)	24. d (pp. 15-16)	34. a (p. 18)
5. d (pp. 5-6)	15. a (p. 12)	25. b (p. 17)	35. d (p. 19)
6. b (p. 7)	16. c (p. 12)	26. c (p. 18)	36. c (p. 19)
7. c (p. 8)	17. c (p. 13)	27. d (p. 18)	37. d (p. 20)
8. a (p. 8)	18. b (p. 13)	28. a (p. 18)	38. e (p. 21)
9. b (p. 8)	19. c (p. 14)	29. b (p. 18)	39. c (p. 21)
10. a (p. 10)	20. e (p. 15)	30. c (p. 18)	40. d (p. 25)

Matching

Perspective and Theory:

1. i (p. 8)	4. l (p. 10)	7. j (p. 12)	9. c (p. 13)
2. g (p. 8)	5. b (p. 12)	8. h (p. 13)	10. p (p. 14)
3. k (p. 10)	6. m (p. 12)		

Methods:

1. j (p. 15)	4. g (p. 18)	7. a (p. 21)	9. c (p. 22)
2. d (p. 17)	5. i (p. 18)	8. e (p 22)	10. f (p. 23)
3. h (p. 18)	6. b (p. 18)		

Fill-in-the-blank

1. sociology (p. 3)
2. integration (p. 5)

3. global perspective (p. 8)
4. high (p. 8)
5. interconnected, serious, ourselves (pp. 8-10)
6. industrial technology, cities, political (pp. 10-11)
7. theological, metaphysical, scientific (p. 10)
8. theory (p. 12)
9. theoretical paradigm (p. 12)
10. micro-level (p. 14)
11. Empirical (p. 15)
12. Measurement (p. 18)
13. Correlation (p. 18)
14. objectivity (p. 18)
15. Max Weber (p. 18)
16. Interpretive (p. 19)
17. Critical (p. 19)
18. androcentricity, overgeneralizing, blindness, double, interference (pp. 20-21)
19. survey (p. 21)
20. sample (p. 22)
21. questionnaires, interviews (p. 22)
22. stereotype (p. 25)

PART VII: IN FOCUS—MAJOR ISSUES

1. Illustrate each of the following major components of the *sociological perspective:*
    A. Seeing the general in the particular

    B. Seeing the strange in the familiar

    C. Seeing individuality in social context

2. What are the four *benefits of the sociological perspective?*

3. What are three reasons why *global perspective* is so important today?

4. Identify the major concepts and dominant viewpoint for each of the following *theoretical paradigms:*
    A. Structural-Functional

    B. Social-Conflict

    C. Symbolic-Interaction

5. Describe the perspective offered by each of the following *sociological frameworks* using either divorce or unemployment to illustrate each framework:
    A. Scientific Sociology

    B. Interpretive Sociology

C. Critical Sociology

6. Explain what is meant by the *ideal of objectivity*:

7. Briefly describe each of the following *research designs* used by sociologists:
   A. Experiment

   B. Survey

   C. Participant Observation

   D. Existing Sources

8. What three factors need to be known to be sure *cause-and-effect* exists?

9. Outline and describe the *ten steps in the sociological research process*:

Society: The Basics, Second Canadian Edition

PART VIII: ANALYSIS AND COMMENT

Go back through the chapter and write down key points from each of the following boxes. Then, for each of the boxes identified, write out three questions concerning the issues raised which you feel would be valuable to discuss in class. Do the same for each chapter as you read through the text.

Social Diversity
"What's in a Name? How Social Forces Affect Personal Choice"

Key Points: Questions:

Window on the World – Global Map 1-1
"Economic Development in Global Perspective"

Key Points: Questions:

Critical Thinking
"Sports: Playing the Theory Game"

Key Points: Questions:

Social Diversity
"Conducting Research with Minorities"

Key Points: Questions:

Controversy and Debate
"Is Sociology Nothing More than Stereotypes?"

Key Points: Questions:

Culture

PART I: CHAPTER OUTLINE
1. What is Culture?
    A. Culture and Human Intelligence
2. The Components of Culture
    A. Symbols
    B. Language
    C. Values and Beliefs
    D. Canadian Values
    E. Norms
    F. "Ideal" and "Real" Culture
3. Technology and Culture
    A. Hunting and Gathering
    B. Horticulture and Pastoralism
    C. Agriculture
    D. Industry
    E. Post-industrial Information Technology
4. Cultural Diversity
    A. High Culture and Popular Culture
    B. Subculture
    C. Multiculturalism
    D. Counterculture
    E. Cultural Change
    F. Ethnocentrism and Cultural Relativity
    G. A Global Culture?
5. Theoretical Analysis of Culture
    A. Structural-Functional Analysis
    B. Social-Conflict Analysis
    C. Sociobiology: Where Biology Meets Culture
6. Culture and Human Freedom
7. Summary
8. Key Concepts
9. Critical-Thinking Questions
10. Applications and Exercises
11. Sites to See

21

PART II: LEARNING OBJECTIVES

1. To begin to understand the sociological meaning of the concept of culture.
2. To consider the relationship between human intelligence and culture.
3. To know the components of culture and to be able to provide examples of each.
4. To consider the current state of knowledge about whether language is uniquely human.
5. To consider the significance of symbols in the construction and maintenance of social reality.
6. To identify the dominant values in our society and to recognize their interrelationships with one another and with other aspects of our culture.
7. To be able to provide examples of the different types of norms operative in a culture, and how these are related to the process of social control.
8. To be able to identify and describe the different types of societies as distinguished by their level of technology.
9. To be able to explain how subcultures and countercultures contribute to cultural diversity.
10. To begin to develop your understanding of multiculturalism.
11. To be able to differentiate between ethnocentrism and cultural relativism.
12. To be able to compare and contrast analyses of culture using structural-functional, social-conflict, and sociobiological paradigms.
13. To be able to identify the consequences of culture for human freedom and constraint.

PART III: KEY CONCEPTS

beliefs

agriculture

counterculture

cultural integration

cultural lag

cultural relativism

cultural transmission

cultural universals

culture

culture shock

ethnocentrism

Eurocentrism

folkways

high culture

horticulture

hunting and gathering

industry

language

multiculturalism

norms

pastoralism

popular culture

Sapir-Whorf thesis

society

sociobiology

subculture

symbol

technology

values

PART IV: IMPORTANT RESEARCHERS

Napoleon Chagnon   John Porter

Edward Sapir and Benjamin Whorf

Society: The Basics, Second Canadian Edition

PART V: STUDY QUESTIONS
True-False

1. T F *Individualism* is even more valued in Japan than in Canada.
2. T F *Nonmaterial culture* refers to the intangible world of ideas created by members of a society.
3. T F No way of life is "natural" to humanity, even though most people around the world view their own behaviour that way.
4. T F The term *society* refers to a shared way of life.
5. T F According to the evolutionary record, the human line diverged from our closest primate relative, the great apes, some *12 million years ago*.
6. T F Cultural *symbols* can vary within a single society.
7. T F *Cultural transmission* is defined as the process by which one generation passes on culture to the next.
8. T F The *Sapir-Whorf thesis* concerns the extent to which the dominant values of a culture are affected by its level of technological development.
9. T F *Values* are defined as rules and expectations by which society guides the behaviour of its members.
10. T F *Mores* are norms which have little moral significance within a culture.
11. T F *Technology* is defined as the knowledge that people apply to the task of living in their surroundings.
12. T F *Horticulture* refers to the use of hand-tools to raise crops.
13. T F *Hunting and gathering societies* tend to be characterized by more social inequality than horticultural or agrarian societies.
14. T F *Agrarian societies* emerged about 5 000 years ago.
15. T F *Virtual culture* refers to the gap between "ideal" and "real" culture.
16. T F Compared to Japan, Canada is a very *monocultural* nation.
17. T F During the last decade, most *immigrants* to Canada have come from Asia and Latin America.
18. T F *Subcultures* involve not just differences but hierarchy.
19. T F *Multiculturalism* refers to an educational program recognizing the cultural diversity of Canada and promoting the equality of all cultural traditions.
20. T F Three major sources of cultural change are *invention, discovery,* and *diffusion*.
21. T F The practice of judging any culture by its own standards is referred to as *ethnocentrism*.
22. T F *Structural-functionalists* argue that there are no *cultural universals*.
23. T F *Sociobiology* rests on the theory of evolution as proposed by Charles Darwin.
24. T F According to the authors of our text, culture has diminished human autonomy to the point where we are *culturally programmed* much like other animals are *genetically programmed*.

Multiple-Choice

1. *Culture* is
   a) the process by which members of a culture encourage conformity to social norms.
   b) the beliefs, values, behaviour, and material objects that constitute a people's way of life.
   c) the practice of judging another society's norms.
   d) a group of people who engage in interaction with one another on a continuous basis.
   e) the aspects of social life people admire most.

2. The personal disorientation that accompanies exposure to an unfamiliar way of life is termed
   a) anomie.
   b) alienation.
   c) cultural relativism.
   d) culture shock.
   e) cultural transmission.

3. The organized interaction of people in a nation or within some other boundary is the definition for
   a) culture.
   b) social structure.
   c) society.
   d) socialization.
   e) acculturation.

4. _____ set(s) humans apart from other primates.
   a) Our sociability
   b) Our affectionate and long-lasting bonds for child rearing and mutual protection
   c) Our ability to walk upright
   d) Our hands that manipulate objects with great precision
   e) None of the above

5. The *Yąnomamö* are
   a) a small tribal group of herders living in Eastern Africa.
   b) a technologically primitive horticultural society living in South America.
   c) a nomadic culture living above the Arctic circle as hunters.
   d) a small, dying society living as farmers in a mountainous region of western Africa.
   e) a people who until very recently were living in complete isolation from the rest of the world in a tropical rain forest in Malaysia.

6. Studying *fossil records*, scientists have concluded that the first creatures with clearly human characteristics existed about _____ years ago.
   a) 3 million
   b) 12 thousand
   c) 40 million
   d) 60 thousand
   e) 12 million

7. *Homo sapiens* is a Latin term that means
   a) thinking person.
   b) to walk upright.
   c) evolving life form.
   d) dependent person.

8. Which of the following identifies two of the *components of culture*?
   a) values and norms
   b) social change and social statics
   c) social structure and social function
   d) people and the natural environment

9. *Symbols*, a component of culture, can
   a) vary from culture to culture.
   b) provide a foundation for the reality we experience.
   c) vary within a given culture.
   d) all of the above

10. The *language* that is the native tongue of twenty percent of the world's population (more than any other language) is
    a) English.
    b) Chinese.
    c) Spanish.
    d) Arabic.

11. A system of *symbols* that allows members of a society to communicate with one other is the definition of
    a) language.
    b) cultural relativity.
    c) cultural transmission.
    d) values.
    e) norms.

12. The *Sapir-Whorf thesis* relates to
    a) human evolution.
    b) language and cultural relativity.
    c) social sanctions.
    d) victimization patterns.

13. The process by which one generation passes culture on to the next refers to
    a) cultural transmission.
    b) sociocultural evolution.
    c) cultural relativism
    d) ethnocentrism.

14. Culturally defined *standards* of desirability, goodness, and beauty, which serve as broad guidelines for social living, is the definition for
    a) norms.
    b) mores.
    c) beliefs.
    d) sanctions.
    e) values.

15. Specific statements that people hold to be true refers to
    a) values.
    b) norms.
    c) structures.
    d) sanctions.
    e) beliefs.

16. *Equity* and *fairness* are examples of important _____ in Canada.
    a) norms
    b) sanctions
    c) values
    d) beliefs

17. According to the research cited in the text, which of the following is *not* a central cultural value in Canada?
    a) support for diversity
    b) compassion and generosity
    c) attachment to Canada's natural beauty
    d) importance of military in protecting our sovereignty
    e) consultation and dialogue

18. Rules and expectations by which a society guides the behaviour of is members refers to
    a) norms.
    b) values.
    c) sanctions.
    d) beliefs.

19. The old adage "Do as I say, not as I do" illustrates the distinction between
    a) folkways and mores.
    b) the Sapir-Whorf hypothesis.
    c) cultural integration and cultural lag.
    d) ideal and real culture.
    e) subcultures and countercultures.

20. *Tangible* human creations are called
    a) technology.
    b) values.
    c) artifacts.
    d) real culture.

21. Knowledge that people apply to the task of living in their surroundings refers to
    a) social control.
    b) technology.
    c) real culture.
    d) ideal culture.

22. Gerhard and Jean Lenski focus on which factor as a major determinant of social change?
    a) human ideas
    b) technology
    c) social solidarity
    d) religious doctrine

23. The concept of *sociocultural evolution* focuses our attention on _____ as a key in cultural change.
    a) technology
    b) values
    c) beliefs
    d) sanctions

24. The key organizational principle of *hunting and gathering* societies is
    a) politics.
    b) religion.
    c) health.
    d) kinship.

25. Which of the following qualities is/are more characteristic of *horticultural* and *agrarian* societies as compared to hunting and gathering societies?
    a) greater social inequality
    b) greater material surplus
    c) greater specialization
    d) all of the above

26. *Agrarian societies* first emerged about _____ years ago.
    a) 1000
    b) 12 000
    c) 25 000
    d) 50 000
    e) 5 000

27. *Post-industrial society* is _____-based.
    a) family
    b) labour and work
    c) gender
    d) leisure
    e) ideas and information

28. Cultural patterns that distinguish a society's *elite* refer to
    a) popular culture.
    b) high culture.
    c) affluent culture.
    d) prestige culture.
    e) counterculture.

29. Cultural patterns that set apart some segment of a society's population is termed
    a) social stratification.
    b) social differentiation.
    c) counterculture.
    d) cultural lag.
    e) subculture.

30. Canadian culture is best viewed as a
    a) melting pot.
    b) mosaic.
    c) single culture.
    d) counter culture.

31. Critics of multiculturalism argue that it
    a) enables students to understand our homogenous population.
    b) teaches people to live in a world where nations are increasingly isolated.
    c) empowers minorities.
    d) erodes any claim for universal truths and our common humanity.

32. Inconsistencies within a cultural system resulting from the unequal rates at which different cultural elements change is termed
    a) cultural lag.
    b) counterculture.
    c) culture shock.
    d) cultural relativity.
    e) ethnocentrism.

33. The spread of cultural elements from one society to another is called
    a) invention.
    b) integration.
    c) diffusion.
    d) discovery.

34. *Ethnocentrism* is:
    a) an educational program recognizing past and present cultural diversity
    b) cultural patterns that set apart some segment of society's population
    c) cultural patterns that strongly oppose those widely accepted within a society
    d) the practice of judging another culture by the standards of one's own culture
    e) the practice of judging another culture by its own standards

35. The theoretical paradigm that focuses upon *universal cultural traits* is
    a) cultural ecology.
    b) structural-functionalism.
    c) cultural materialism.
    d) social-conflict.

36. The philosophical doctrine of *materialism* is utilized in the analysis of culture by proponents of which theoretical paradigm?
    a) sociobiologists
    b) cultural ecology
    c) social-conflict
    d) structural-functionalism

Matching

1. _____ The intangible world of ideas created by members of society.
2. _____ Anything that carries a particular meaning recognized by people who share a culture.
3. _____ The official language of twenty percent of the world's population.
4. _____ States that people perceive the world through the cultural lens of language.
5. _____ Rules and expectations by which a society guides the behaviour of its members.
6. _____ Knowledge that a people apply to the task of living in their surroundings.
7. _____ The use of hand tools to raise crops.
8. _____ An educational program recognizing past and present diversity in Canadian society and promoting the equality of all cultural traditions.
9. _____ Cultural patterns that strongly oppose those widely accepted within a society.
10. _____ The fact that cultural elements change at different rates, which may disrupt a cultural system.
11. _____ The practice of judging another culture by the standards of one's own culture.
12. _____ A theoretical paradigm that explores ways in which biology affects how humans create culture.

a. horticulture
b. sociobiology
c. counterculture
d. cultural lag
e. Sapir-Whorf thesis
f. ethnocentrism
g. nonmaterial culture
h. multiculturalism
i. Chinese
j. technology
k. norms
l. symbol
m. mores
n. English
o. agriculture

Study Guide

Fill-in-the-blank

1. The 6.2 billion people on earth today are members of a single biological species: _____ _____.

2. _____ are the biological programming over which animals have no control.

3. The *tangible things* created by members of society are referred to as _____ _____.

4. The concept _____ _____ is derived from the Latin meaning *thinking person*.

5. Four key *components of culture* include: _____, _____, _____, and _____.

6. Anything that carries a particular meaning recognized by people who share culture refers to _____.

7. Culture shock is both _____ and _____ by the traveller.

8. The two most widely spoken languages in the world are _____, and _____.

9. The process by which one generation passes culture to the next refers to _____ _____.

10. Specific statements that people hold to be true are _____.

11. While _____ are culturally defined standards of desirability, goodness, and beauty that serve as broad guidelines for social living, _____ are specific statements that people hold to be true.

12. _____ are rules and expectations by which a society guides the behaviour of its members.

13. _____ refers to knowledge that people apply to the task of living in their surroundings.

14. _____ refers to large-scale cultivation using plows harnessed to animals or more powerful energy sources.

31

15. _____ *culture* refers to cultural patterns widespread among a society's population.

16. _____ is an educational program recognizing the cultural diversity of Canada and promoting the equality of all cultural traditions.

17. The fact that some cultural elements change more quickly than others, which may disrupt a cultural system, refers to _____ _____.

18. _____ refers to the practice of judging another culture by the standards of one's own culture.

19. The _____-_____ *paradigm* depicts culture as a complex strategy for meeting human needs. Borrowing from the philosophical doctrine of *idealism*, this approach views values at the core of culture.

20. *Social conflict theory* is rooted in the philosophical doctrine of _____ which holds that a society's system of material production has a powerful effect on the rest of culture.

21. _____ is a theoretical paradigm that studies the ways in which human biology affects the way we create culture.

Definition and Short-Answer

1. Three *causes of cultural change* are identified in the text. Identify these and provide an illustration of each.
2. Review the list of Canadian values listed on page 36. What contradictions do you witness in your daily life? To what extent do your interpretation of Canadian values contradict those on the list?
3. What are the basic qualities of the *Yąnomamö* culture? What factors do you think may explain why they are so aggressive? To what extent are you able to view these people from a *cultural relativistic* perspective?
4. What is the basic position being taken by *sociobiologists* concerning the nature of culture? What are three arguments or examples used by sociobiologists to argue that human culture is determined by biology? To what extent do you agree or disagree with their position? Explain.
5. What is the *Sapir-Whorf thesis*? What evidence supports it? What evidence is inconsistent with this hypothesis?

6. Write a paragraph in which you express your opinions about the issue of multiculturalism in our society. Address the benefits of this perspective being suggested by proponents of multiculturalism, as well as the potential problems with this perspective suggested by its critics.
7. How do the Lenskis define *sociocultural evolution*?
8. What are the basic *types of societies* based on level of technological development? What are three important characteristics of each type of society?
9. Provide two examples of how culture *constrains* us (limits our freedom).
10. Differentiate between *values* and *norms*, providing two illustrations for each.
11. Review the list of *core values* of our culture in Canada. Rank order the seven identified in the text in terms of how important they are in our society from your point of view. What values, if any, do you believe should be included in the "top ten" list? Do you feel any of those listed should not be on the list?

PART VI: ANSWERS TO STUDY QUESTIONS

True-False
1. F (p. 30)
2. T (p. 30)
3. T (p. 30)
4. F (p. 30)
5. T (p. 31)
6. T (p. 35)
7. T (p. 35)
8. F (p. 35)
9. F (p. 36)
10. F (p. 36)
11. T (p. 37)
12. T (p. 38)
13. F (p. 38)
14. T (p. 38)
15. F (p. 40)
16. F (p. 41)
17. T (p. 41)
18. T (p. 42)
19. T (p. 43)
20. T (p. 46)
21. F (p. 46)
22. F (p. 48)
23. T (p. 50)
24. F (p. 51)

Multiple Choice
1. b (p. 30)
2. d (p. 30)
3. c (p. 30)
4. e (p. 32)
5. b (p. 32)
6. a (p. 32)
7. a (p. 32)
8. a (p. 33)
9. d (pp. 33-35)
10. b (p. 34)
11. a (p. 35)
12. b (p. 35)
13. a (p. 35)
14. e (p. 36)
15. e (p. 36)
16. c (p. 36)
17. d (p. 36)
18. a (p. 36)
19. d (p. 37)
20. c (p. 37)
21. b (p. 37)
22. b (p. 37)
23. a (p. 37)
24. d (p. 37)
25. d (pp. 37-39)
26. e (p. 38)
27. e (p. 41)
28. b (p. 41)
29. e (p. 42)
30. b (p. 42)
31. d (pp. 43-44)
32. a (p. 45)
33. c (p. 46)
34. d (p. 46)
35. b (p. 48)
36. c (p. 49)

Matching
1. g (p. 30)
2. l (p. 33)
3. i (p. 34)
4. e (p. 35)
5. k (p. 36)
6. j (p. 37)
7. a (p. 37)
8. h (p. 43)
9. c (p. 44)
10. d (p. 45)
11. f (p. 46)
12. b (p. 50)

Fill-in-the-blank
1. homo sapiens (p. 29)
2. Instincts (p. 30)
3. material culture (p. 30)
4. homo sapiens (p. 32)
5. symbols, language, values, norms (p. 33)
6. symbol (p. 33)
7. experienced, inflicted (p. 33)

Society: The Basics, Second Canadian Edition

8. Chinese (Mandarin), English (p. 34)
9. cultural transmission (p. 35)
10. beliefs (p. 36)
11. values, beliefs (p. 36)
12. Norms (p. 36)
13. Technology (p. 37)
14. Agriculture (p. 38)
15. Popular (p. 41)
16. Multiculturalism (p. 43)
17. Cultural lag (p. 45)
18. Ethnocentrism (p. 46)
19. Structural-functionalism (p. 48)
20. materialism (p. 49)
21. Sociobiology (p. 50)

PART VII: IN FOCUS—MAJOR ISSUES

1. Define and illustrate the concepts of *material* and *nonmaterial culture*.

2. Define and illustrate each of the following four *components of nonmaterial culture*.
   A. Symbols

   B. Language

   C. Values

   D. Norms

3. Identify and illustrate the seven *dominant Canadian values* listed in the text.

4. Describe the major characteristics of societies operating at each of the following levels of *sociocultural evolution*.
    A. Hunting and gathering

    B. Horticultural and Pastoral

    C. Agricultural

    D. Industry

    E. Post-industrial

5. Identify, define, and illustrate three examples of *cultural diversity*.

6. What are three examples of evidence that a *global culture* exists?

7. Briefly identify the basic arguments being made about culture by theorists using each of the following three *theoretical paradigms*.
    A. Structural-Functional Paradigm

    B. Social-Conflict Paradigm

    C. Sociobiology

PART VIII: ANALYSIS AND COMMENT

Global Sociology
"Confronting the Yąnomamö: The Experience of Culture Shock"
Key Points: Questions:

Window on the World—Global Map 2-1
"Language in Global Perspective"
Key Points: Questions:

Critical Thinking
"Virtual Culture: Is It Good for Us?"
Key Points: Questions:

Social Diversity
"Language Rights in Canada: Unifying or Divisive?"
Key Points: Questions:

Society: The Basics, Second Canadian Edition

Seeing Ourselves – National Map 2-1
"Non-Official Home Languages Across Canada, 1996"

Key Points: Questions:

Applying Sociology
"Masculinity as Context"

Key Points: Questions:

Socialization: From Infancy to Old Age

PART I: CHAPTER OUTLINE
1. Social Experience: The Key to Our Humanity
    A. Human Development: Nature and Nurture
    B. Social Isolation
2. Understanding Socialization
    A. Sigmund Freud: The Elements of Personality
    B. Jean Piaget: Cognitive Development
    C. Lawrence Kohlberg: Moral Development
    D. Carol Gilligan: The Gender Factor
    E. George Herbert Mead: The Social Self
3. Agents of Socialization
    A. The Family
    B. The School
    C. The Peer Group
    D. The Mass Media
4. Socialization and the Life Course
    A. Childhood
    B. Adolescence
    C. Adulthood
    D. Old Age
    E. Socialization across the Life Course: An Overview
5. Resocialization: Total Institutions
6. Summary
7. Key Concepts
8. Critical-Thinking Questions
9. Applications and Exercises
10. Sites to See

Society: The Basics, Second Canadian Edition

PART II: LEARNING OBJECTIVES

1. To understand the "nature-nurture" debate regarding socialization and personality development.
2. To become aware of the effects of social isolation on humans and other primates.
3. To become aware of the key components of Sigmund Freud's model of personality.
4. be able to identify and describe the four stages of Jean Piaget's cognitive development theory.
5. To be able to identify and describe the stages of moral development as identified by Lawrence Kohlberg.
6. To analyse Carol Gilligan's critique of Kohlberg's moral development model.
7. To consider the contributions of George Herbert Mead to the understanding of personality development.
8. To be able to compare the spheres of socialization (family, school, etc.) in terms of their effects on an individual's socialization experiences.
9. To develop a life-course perspective of the socialization experience.
10. To be able to discuss the sociological perspective on socialization as a constraint to freedom.

PART III: KEY CONCEPTS

ageism

anticipatory socialization

cohort

concrete operational stage

ego

formal operational stage

hidden curriculum

id

gerontology

gerontocracy

looking-glass self

mass media

peer group

personality

preoperational stage

resocialization

self

sensorimotor stage

socialization

superego

total institution

PART IV: IMPORTANT RESEARCHERS

Kingsley Davis   Lawrence Kohlberg

John B. Watson   Carol Gilligan

Harry and Margaret Harlow   George Herbert Mead

Sigmund Freud   Charles Horton Cooley

Jean Piaget

Society: The Basics, Second Canadian Edition

PART V: STUDY QUESTIONS

True-False

1. T F As defined by our authors, the concept of *personality* does not concern actual behaviour.
2. T F John B. Watson was a nineteenth-century psychologist who argued that human behaviour was largely determined by *heredity*.
3. T F The Harlows' research on rhesus monkeys concerning *social isolation* illustrates that while short-term isolation can be overcome, long-term isolation appears to cause irreversible emotional and behavioural damage to monkeys.
4. T F The cases of *Isabelle, Anna,* and *Genie* support the arguments made by naturalists that certain personality characteristics are determined by heredity.
5. T F *Socialization* is a complex, lifelong process.
6. T F Sigmund Freud envisioned *biological factors* as having little or no influence on personality development.
7. T F The *id* in Freud's psychoanalytic theory represents the human being's basic needs which are unconscious and demand immediate satisfaction.
8. T F The first stage in Jean Piaget's *cognitive development theory* is referred to as the *preoperational stage*.
9. T F According to Jean Piaget, language and other symbols are first used in the *preoperational stage*.
10. T F While Sigmund Freud saw human beings torn by opposing forces of biology and culture, Jean Piaget saw the mind as active and creative.
11. T F According to Lawrence Kohlberg, during the *preconventional stage* of moral development, a person defines "rightness" in terms of "what feels good to me."
12. T F Carol Gilligan's research focusses on how *gender* affects *moral reasoning*.
13. T F According to Carol Gilligan, taking a *rule-based approach* to moral reasoning is superior to taking a *person-based approach*.
14. T F George Herbert Mead argued that *biological factors* played *little or no* role in the development of the self.
15. T F George Herbert Mead refers to *taking the role of the other* as the interplay between the *I* and *me*.
16. T F George Herbert Mead's concept of the *generalized other* refers to widespread cultural norms and values shared by us and others that we use as a reference point to evaluate ourselves.
17. T F According to George Herbert Mead, the objective side of the self is known as the *me*.
18. T F The concept *hidden curriculum* relates to the important cultural values being transmitted to children in school.

19. T F A *peer group* is a social group whose members have interests, social positions, and age in common.
20. T F More than half Canadian households have at least two televisions sets.
21. T F The percentage of our society's population over the age of sixty-five has been *declining* over the last several decades.
22. T F The study of childhood is known as *gerontology*.
23. T F A *cohort* is a setting in which people are isolated from the rest of society and manipulated by an administrative staff.
24. T F *Resocialization* is a straightforward process that changes personality by building on pre-existing strengths and weaknesses.

Multiple Choice

1. The story of *Anna* illustrates the significance of _____ in personality development.
   a) heredity
   b) social interaction
   c) physical conditions
   d) ecology

2. The lifelong social experience by which individuals develop their human potential and learn culture is called
   a) socialization.
   b) personality.
   c) adjustment.
   d) adaptation.
   e) behaviourism.

3. A person's fairly constant patterns of acting, thinking, and feeling is called
   a) socialization.
   b) personality.
   c) behaviourism.
   d) reasoning.

4. The perspective developed by the psychologist John B. Watson, claiming that human behaviour is not instinctive, but learned within a social environment, is termed
   a) naturalism.
   b) psychology.
   c) sociology.
   d) evolution.
   e) behaviourism.

5. The major tenet of *behaviourism* is that
   a) behaviour patterns are instinctive, not learned.
   b) behaviour patterns are learned, not instinctive.
   c) humans are culturally similar around the world.
   d) feelings and thoughts connected to behaviours are more important than the behaviours themselves.

6. What did the experiments on social isolation among rhesus monkeys show?
   a) Artificial wire-mesh monkeys provided sufficient contact for young monkeys to develop normally.
   b) The behaviour of rhesus monkey infants is totally dissimilar to human infants.
   c) Deprivation of social experience, rather than the absence of a specific parent, has devastating effects.
   d) Biological forces in rhesus monkeys cushions them from the negative effects of social isolation.

7. Which of the following is representative of *Sigmund Freud's* analysis of personality?
   a) Biological forces play only a small role in personality development.
   b) The term instinct is understood as very general human needs in the form of urges and drives.
   c) The most significant period for personality development is adolescence.
   d) Personality is best studied as a process of externalizing social forces.

8. *Sigmund Freud's* model of personality does *not* include which of the following elements?
   a) superego
   b) id
   c) self
   d) ego

9. Culture existing within the individual *Sigmund Freud* called
   a) thanatos.
   b) eros.
   c) the ego.
   d) the id.
   e) the superego.

10. In Sigmund Freud's model of personality, what balances the innate pleasure-seeking drive with the demands of society?
    a) id
    b) ego
    c) superego
    d) thanatos

11. According to *Jean Piaget*, which of the following best describes the *preoperational stage* of cognitive development?
    a) the level of human development in which the world is experienced only through sensory contact
    b) the level of human development characterized by the use of logic to understand objects and events
    c) the level of human development in which language and other symbols are first used
    d) the level of human development characterized by highly abstract thought

12. Jean Piaget's focus was on
    a) how children develop fine motor skills.
    b) how children are stimulated by their environment.
    c) cognition–how people think and understand.
    d) role of heredity in determining human behaviour.

13. According to *Jean Piaget's* cognitive development theory, the _____ stage refers to a level of development at which individuals first perceive causal connections in their surroundings.
    a) preoperational
    b) conventional
    c) play
    d) concrete operational

14. In *Lawrence Kohlberg's* moral development theory the _____ level refers to the period during which people shed some of their selfishness as they learn to define right and wrong in terms of what pleases parents and what fits with cultural norms.
    a) conventional
    b) preconventional
    c) postconventional
    d) operational
    e) imitative

15. According to research by *Carol Gilligan*, males use a _____ perspective concerning moral reasoning.
    a) justice
    b) independent
    c) visual
    d) mechanical

16. *George Herbert Mead's* perspective has often been described as
    a) psychological pragmatism.
    b) behaviourism.
    c) social behaviourism.
    d) psychoanalysis.
    e) naturalism.

17. According to *George Herbert Mead*, all symbolic interaction involves seeing ourselves as others see us—a process he called _____.
    a) repression
    b) taking the role of the other
    c) imitation
    d) cognition
    e) sublimation

18. The first stage in *George Herbert Mead's* developmental theory of the social self is
    a) play.
    b) imitation.
    c) game.
    d) play.

45

19. George Herbert Mead used the term _____ to describe the widespread cultural norms and values shared by us and others that we use as a point of reference in evaluating ourselves.
    a) looking-glass self
    b) socialization
    c) significant other
    d) generalized other

20. The concept of the *looking-glass self* refers to
    a) Freud's argument that through psychoanalysis a person can uncover the unconscious.
    b) Piaget's view that through biological maturation and social experience individuals become able to logically hypothesize about thoughts without relying on concrete reality.
    c) Watson's behaviourist notion that one can see through to a person's mind only by observing the person's behaviour.
    d) Cooley's idea that the self-image we have is based on how we suppose others perceive us.

21. For most individuals, _____ has the greatest impact on socialization.
    a) peers
    b) the family
    c) teachers
    d) mass media
    e) the internet

22. The _____ allows children to escape the direct supervision of adults.
    a) family
    b) school
    c) peer group
    d) mass media

23. The generation gap is often separate the attitudes of
    a) parents and children.
    b) school and children.
    c) peer groups and children.
    d) religion and children.

24. The process of social learning directed toward assuming a desired status and role in the future is called
    a) resocialization.
    b) socialization.
    c) looking-glass self.
    d) anticipatory socialization.

25. The _____ are impersonal communications directed at a vast audience.
    a) mass media
    b) total institution
    c) hidden curriculum
    d) generalized other
    e) 54

26. On average Canadian viewers watch television an average of about ___ hours each week.
    a) 10
    b) 20
    c) 30
    d) 40
    e) 50

27. Which of the following is *not* one of the three distinctive characteristics of a *total institution*?
    a) staff members supervise all spheres of daily life
    b) staff members encourage the maintenance of individuality, and encourage creativity
    c) food, sleeping quarters and activities are standardized
    d) formal rules dictate how virtually every moment is spent

28. _____ refers to a process of radically altering the personality through deliberate manipulation of the environment.
    a) Anticipatory socialization
    b) Resocialization
    c) Primary socialization
    d) Degradation

Matching

1. ____ A person's fairly consistent patterns of acting, thinking, and feeling.
2. ____ The operation of culture within the individual.
3. ____ Deliberate socialization intended to radically alter the individual's personality.
4. ____ A category of people with a common characteristic, usually their age.
5. ____ The self-image we have based on how we suppose others perceive us.
6. ____ A group whose members have interests, social position, and age in common.
7. ____ A theory developed by John B. Watson that holds that behaviour patterns are not instinctive but learned.
8. ____ A setting in which individuals are isolated from the rest of society and manipulated by an administrative staff.
9. ____ Impersonal communications directed to a vast audience.
10. ____ In Piaget's theory, the level of development at which individuals perceive causal connections in their surroundings.
11. ____ According to George Herbert Mead, the subjective side of the self.
12. ____ Prejudice and discrimination against the elderly.

a. looking-glass self
b. behaviourism
c. mass media
d. concrete operational stage
e. resocialization
f. superego
g. cohort
h. peer group
i. personality
j. total institution
k. me
l. I
m. negotiation
n. ageism

Society: The Basics, Second Canadian Edition

Fill-in-the-blank

1. _____ is defined as a person's fairly consistent pattern of acting, thinking, and feeling.

2. The approach called _____ developed by *John B. Watson* in the early twentieth century provided a perspective that stressed learning rather than instincts as the key to personality development.

3. According to *Sigmund Freud*, the _____ represents a person's conscious efforts to balance the innate pleasure-seeking drives of the human organism and the demands of society.

4. *Sigmund Freud* argued that culture, in the form of the superego serves to _____, whereas he called the process of transforming fundamentally selfish drives into more socially acceptable objectives _____.

5. *Jean Piaget's* work centred on human _____.

6. *Lawrence Kohlberg* identifies three stages in moral development, including the _____, the _____, and the _____.

7. *Carol Gilligan* suggests that boys tend to use a *justice perspective* in moral reasoning, relying on formal rules in reaching a judgment about right and wrong. On the other hand, says Gilligan, girls tend to use a _____ and _____ *perspective* in moral reasoning, which leads them to judge a situation with an eye toward personal relationships.

8. *George Herbert Mead* explained that infants with limited social experience respond to others only in terms of _____.

9. Some critics say Mead/s view is completely social, whereas _____ identified general human drives, and _____ whose stages of development are tied to biological maturation.

10. The process of social learning directed toward gaining a desired position is called _____ *socialization*.

48

11. Impersonal communications directed to a vast audience refers to the _____ _____.

12. A _____ is a form of social organization in which the elderly have the most wealth, power, and privileges.

13. The _____ Generation is a label given to those who care for a child at home while they at the same time have elderly parents to care for.

14. Prisons and mental hospitals are examples of _____ _____.

Definition and Short-Answer

1. How did the work of *Charles Darwin* influence the understanding of personality development in the late nineteenth century?
2. What was *John B. Watson's* view concerning personality development?
3. Review the research by *Harry* and *Margaret Harlow* on social isolation. What were the important discoveries they made?
4. Discuss the cases of *childhood isolation* presented in the text. What are the important conclusions being drawn from these cases?
5. Identify and define the parts of personality as seen by *Sigmund Freud*.
6. What are the four stages of cognitive development according to *Jean Piaget*? Briefly describe the qualities of each stage. What is one major criticism of his theory?
7. Define the concept *looking-glass self*. Provide an illustration of this concept from your own personal experience.
8. Define and differentiate between the terms *generalized other* and *significant other*. Further, what are the four basic arguments being made by *George Herbert Mead* concerning personality development?
9. According to the text, what are the four important *agents of socialization*? Provide an illustration of how each is involved in the socialization process.
10. What are the stages of *adulthood* and the qualities of each?
11. What is a *total institution*? What are the typical experiences of a person who is living within a total institution? How do these experiences affect personality development?
12. Based on the sociological research cited in this chapter, to what extent can it be argued that humans are like "puppets" in society?
13. What conclusions are being made by the author concerning the *life course*?

PART VI: ANSWERS TO STUDY QUESTIONS

True-False
1. F (p. 55)   3. T (p. 57)   5. T (p. 58)   7. T (p. 58)
2. F (p. 56)   4. F (pp.57-58) 6. F (p. 58)   8. F (p. 58)

Society: The Basics, Second Canadian Edition

9. T (p. 58)	13. F (p. 60)	17. T (p. 61)	21. F (p. 68)
10. T (p. 59)	14. T (p. 60)	18. T (p. 62)	22. F (p. 69)
11. T (p. 59)	15. T (p. 61)	19. T (p. 63)	23. F (p. 72)
12. T (p. 60)	16. T (p. 61)	20. T (p. 64)	24. F (p. 72)

Multiple Choice

1. b (p. 55)	8. c (p. 58)	15. a (p. 60)	22. d (p. 63)
2. a (p. 55)	9. e (p. 58)	16. c (p. 60)	23. c (p. 63)
3. b (p. 55)	10. b (p. 58)	17. d (p. 60)	24. d (p. 63)
4. e (p. 56)	11. c (p. 58)	18. b (p. 61)	25. a (p. 63)
5. b (p. 56)	12. c (p. 58)	19. d (p. 61)	26. c (p. 64)
6. c (p. 57)	13. d (p. 59)	20. b (p. 61)	27. b (p. 72)
7. b (p. 58)	14. a (p. 59)	21. d (p. 62)	28. b (p. 72)

Matching

1. i (p. 55)	4. g (p. 72)	7. b (p. 56)	10. d (p. 59)
2. f (p. 58)	5. a (p. 61)	8. e (p. 72)	11. l (p. 61)
3. e (p. 72)	6. h (p. 63)	9. c (p. 63)	12. n (p. 71)

Fill-in-the-blank

1. personality (p. 55)
2. behaviourism (p. 56)
3. ego (p. 58)
4. repress, sublimation (p. 58)
5. cognition (p. 58)
6. preconventional, conventional, postconventional (p. 59)
7. care, responsibility (p. 60)
8. imitation (p. 61)
9. Freud, Piaget (p. 61)
10. anticipatory (p. 63)
11. mass media (p. 63)
12. gerontocracy (p. 70)
13. Sandwich (p. 70)
14. total institutions (p. 72)

PART VII: IN FOCUS—MAJOR ISSUES

1. Review the major points concerning the impact of *social isolation* on human development. Make specific reference to the Harlow's research with monkeys and the research on isolated children.

Study Guide

2. Identify and define the elements of personality according to *Sigmund Freud*.

3. Describe each of the following stages in *Jean Piaget's* cognitive development model.
    A. Sensorimotor

    B. Preoperational

    C. Concrete Operational

    D. Formal Operational

4. Describe each of the three levels of moral development according to *Lawrence Kohlberg*.
    A. Preconventional

    B. Conventional

    C. Postconventional

Society: The Basics, Second Canadian Edition

5. Identify and describe the four major ideas *George Herbert Mead* connected to the concept of *self*.

6. Describe each of the following stages in the developmental theory of *George Herbert Mead*.
    A. Imitation

    B. Play

    C. Game

    D. Generalized Other

7. Review one major point made in the text concerning each of the following *agents of socialization*.

The Family   The School

The Peer Group   The Mass Media

Study Guide

8. Identify two major points made in the text for each of the following periods of socialization in the life course.
   A. Childhood

   B. Adolescence

   C. Adulthood

   D. Old Age

9. What are the three major qualities of a *total institution*?

PART VIII: ANALYSIS AND COMMENT

Social Diversity
"Minority Identity in Movies and Television"
Key Points: Questions:

Window on the World–Global Map 3-1
"Child Labour in Global Perspective"
Key Points: Questions:

53

Society: The Basics, Second Canadian Edition

Seeing Ourselves – National Map 3-1
"Aging Across Canada, 1996"
Key Points: Questions:

Critical Thinking
"The Sandwich Generation: Who Should Care For Aging Parents?"
Key Points: Questions:

Controversy and Debate
"Are Canadians Free within Society"
Key Points: Questions:

Social Interaction In Everyday Life

PART I: CHAPTER OUTLINE

1. Social Structure: A Guide to Everyday Living
2. Status
    A. Ascribed Status and Achieved Status
    B. Master Status
3. Role
    A. Role Conflict and Role Strain
    B. Role Exit
4. The Social Construction of Reality
    A. The Thomas Theorem
    B. Ethnomethodology
    C. Reality-Building: Class and Culture
5. Dramaturgical Analysis: "The Presentation of Self"
    A. Performances
    B. Nonverbal Communication
    C. Gender and Performances
    D. Idealization
    E. Embarrassment and Tact
6. Interaction in Everyday Life: Two Applications
    A. Language: The Gender Issue
    B. Humour: Playing with Reality
7. Summary
8. Key Concepts
9. Critical-Thinking Questions
10. Applications and Exercises
11. Sites to See

PART II: LEARNING OBJECTIVES
1. To be able to identify the characteristics of social structure.
2. To be able to discuss the relationship between social structure and individuality.
3. To be able to distinguish between the different types of statuses and roles.
4. To be able to describe and illustrate the social construction of reality.
5. To begin to see how the technological capacity of a society influences the social construction of reality.
6. To be able to describe and illustrate the approach known as ethnomethodology.
7. To see the importance of performance, nonverbal communication, idealization, and embarrassment to the "presentation of the self."
8. To be able to describe and illustrate dramaturgical analysis.
9. To be able to use gender and humour as illustrations of how people construct meaning in everyday life.

PART III: KEY CONCEPTS

achieved status

ascribed status

dramaturgical analysis

ethnomethodology

master status

nonverbal communication

personal space

presentation of self

role

role conflict

role set

role strain

social interaction

status

status set

social construction of reality

Thomas theorem

PART IV: IMPORTANT RESEARCHERS

Robert Merton   Erving Goffman

Harold Garfinkel   Paul Ekman

PART V: STUDY QUESTIONS

True-False

1. T F A *status* refers to a pattern of expected behaviour for individual members of society.
2. T F Status is not related to social identity.
3. T F A *status set* refers to all statuses a person holds during his or her lifetime.
4. T F Being an honours student, being a spouse, and being a computer programmer are examples of *ascribed statuses*.
5. T F Both *statuses* and *roles* vary by culture.
6. T F *Role strain* refers to the incompatibility among roles corresponding to a single status.
7. T F The phrase *the social construction of reality* relates to the sociologist's view that statuses and roles structure our lives along narrowly delineated paths.
8. T F The *Thomas theorem* states that statuses expand to accommodate the number of roles occupied by the individual holding those statuses.
9. T F For the *ethnomethodologist*, a deliberate lack of social cooperation may lead the researcher to see more clearly the unspoken rules of everyday life.
10. T F According to *Erving Goffman, performances* are very rigidly scripted, leaving virtually no room for individual adaptation.
11. T F Cross-cultural research suggests that culture plays an important part in specifying the situation that trigger a particular emotion.
12. T F According to research on gender and personal performances, men use significantly more space than women.
13. T F Facial expressions are an important form of *body language*.

14. T F According to *Erving Goffman's* research, *tact* is relatively uncommon in our society.

15. T F According to dramaturgical analysis, *embarrassment* causes discomfort for both the presenter and the audience.

16. T F A foundation of *humour* lies in the contrast between two incongruous realities–the *conventional* and *unconventional*.

17. T F One trait of humourous material which appears to be universal is controversy.

18. T F Researcher Christie Davies found ethnic conflict is a driving force behind *humour* almost everywhere.

Multiple-Choice

1. _____ refers to the process by which people act and react in relation to others.
   a) Status
   b) Social interaction
   c) Performance
   d) Role set

2. What is the term for a recognized social position that an individual occupies?
   a) prestige
   b) social power
   c) status
   d) role
   e) dramaturgy

3. A friend of yours is a daughter, mother, sister, friend, employee, and golfer. All these taken together is your friend's
   a) status.
   b) role configuration.
   c) role complex.
   d) status set.

4. Which of the following is *not* a structural component of social interaction?
   a) master status
   b) role
   c) value
   d) role set
   e) ascribed status

5. The term _____ is used to describe the dynamic expression of a status.
   a) master status
   b) role
   c) performance
   d) dramaturgy
   e) nonverbal communication

6. What is the term for a status that has exceptional importance for social identity, often shaping a person's entire life?
   a) role
   b) ascribed status
   c) achieved status
   d) master status

7. What is the term for patterns of expected behaviour attached to a particular status?
   a) role
   b) master status
   c) achieved status
   d) ascribed status

8. A number of roles attached to a *single status* refers to
   a) a role set.
   b) a status set.
   c) a master status.
   d) role conflict.

9. The incompatibility among the roles corresponding to two or more statuses refers to:
   a) role conflict.
   b) role strain.
   c) status overload.
   d) status inconsistency.

10. Which of the following methods of reducing *role strain* is discussed in your text book?
    a) role dissonance
    b) emphatic rejection
    c) non-cognitive dissonance
    d) compartmentalizing roles

11. The process by which individuals creatively shape reality through social interaction is called
    a) reality construction.
    b) the social construction of reality.
    c) creative reality.
    d) interactive reality.

12. The *Thomas theorem* states
    a) roles are only as important as the statuses to which they are attached.
    b) statuses are only as important as the roles on which they are dependent.
    c) the basis of humanity is built upon the dual existence of creativity and conformity.
    d) common sense is only as good as the social structure within which it is embedded.
    e) situations defined as real become real in their consequences.

13. What is the term for the study of the way people make sense of their everyday lives?
    a) naturalism
    b) phenomenology
    c) ethnomethodology
    d) social psychology

14. The approach used by *ethnomethodologists* to study everyday interaction involves
    a) conducting surveys.
    b) unobtrusive observation.
    c) secondary analysis.
    d) breaking rules.
    e) laboratory experiment.

15. The investigation of social interaction in terms of *theatrical performance* is referred to as
    a) ethnomethodology.
    b) dramaturgical analysis.
    c) theatrical analysis.
    d) phenomenology.

16. The process of the *presentation of the self* is also known as
    a) ethnomethodology.
    b) achieved status.
    c) idealization.
    d) ascribed status.
    e) impression management.

17. *Mr. Preedy*, the fictional character introduced in the text, provides an example of
    a) role conflict.
    b) role strain.
    c) nonverbal communication.
    d) status inconsistency.

18. According to Paul Ekman, there are several *universal emotions*. Which of the following is *not* one he has identified?
    a) hope
    b) fear
    c) sadness
    d) happiness

19. What is *demeanour*?
    a) general conduct and deportment
    b) a non-felony crime
    c) a form of mental illness
    d) gender-specific activity

20. Trying to convince others (and perhaps ourselves) that we do reflect ideal cultural standards rather than selfish motives refers to
    a) backstaging.
    b) idealization.
    c) ethnomethodology.
    d) tact.

21. Helping a person to "save face," or avoid embarrassment, is called
    a) diplomacy.
    b) generosity.
    c) altruism.
    d) tact.

22. Which of the following is *not* an example provided in the text to illustrate how *language* functions to define the sexes?
    a) the attention function
    b) the power function
    c) the value function
    d) the affective function

23. *Humour* is generated by
    a) mixing together opposing realities.
    b) miscommunication.
    c) combining embarrassment and tact.
    d) confusing intent and meaning.

24. Research by Deborah Tannen concerning *communication problems* between women and men focuses on the issue of
    a) power.
    b) humour.
    c) language.
    d) tact.
    e) personal space.

25. Which of the following is *inaccurate* concerning humour?
    a) Humour is a universal human trait.
    b) Humour deals with topics that lend themselves to double meanings or controversy.
    c) Every social group considers certain topics too sensitive for humourous treatment.
    d) What is humourous in one society is virtually always humourous in other societies.

26. Which of the following is *not* a *function of humour*?
    a) Humour can be a stimulant to social change.
    b) Humour limits racism and sexism.
    c) Humour can be a safety valve.
    d) Humour can be used as a form of tact.

Society: The Basics, Second Canadian Edition

Matching

1. _____ Expected behaviour of someone who holds a particular status.
2. _____ Incompatibility among roles corresponding to two or more statuses.
3. _____ A social position a person receives at birth or assumes involuntarily later in life.
4. _____ The process by which people act and react in relation to others.
5. _____ The study of the way people make sense of their everyday lives.
6. _____ The investigation of social interaction in terms of theatrical performance.
7. _____ General conduct or deportment.
8. _____ Situations defined as real become real in their consequences.
9. _____ A recognized social position that an individual occupies.
10. _____ Incompatibility among roles corresponding to a single status.

a. ascribed status
b. ethnomethodology
c. Thomas theorem
d. role strain
e. social interaction
f. role
g. demeanor
h. status
i. dramaturgical analysis
j. role conflict

Fill-in-the-blank

1. _____ _____ refers to the process by which people act and react in relation to others.

2. _____ refers to a recognized social position that an individual occupies in society, while _____ refers to patterns of expected behaviours attached to a particular status.

3. An _____ *status* refers to a social position that a person receives at birth or assumes involuntarily later in life.

4. _____ _____ refers to the incompatibility among the roles corresponding to two or more statuses.

5. The _____ _____ states that situations defined as real are real in their consequences.

6. The study of everyday, common-sense understandings that people within a culture have of the world around them is known as _____.

7. _____ *analysis* is the investigation of social interaction in terms of theatrical performance.

8. _____ ____ _____ refers to ways in which individuals, in various settings, attempt to create specific impressions in the minds of others.

9. Props in a doctor's office, like books and framed diplomas, are examples of the _____ *region* of the setting.

10. According to Paul Ekman's cross-cultural studies, there are *six basic emotions* that are universally shared and expressed in similar ways. These include: _____, _____, _____, _____, _____, and _____.

11. According to *Erving Goffman*, _____ refers to general conduct or deportment.

12. When people try to convince others that what they are doing reflects ideal cultural standards rather than less virtuous motives, *Erving Goffman* said they are involved in _____.

13. Language defines men and women differently in at least three ways–in terms of _____, _____, and _____.

14. According to *Deborah Tannen*, women and men use language differently. The problems couples face in communicating is that what one partner _____ by a comment is not always what the other _____.

15. *Humour* stems from the contrast between two incongruous realities, the _____ and the _____.

Definition and Short-Answer

1. Review the illustration of the physician's office and *performances* in the text. Using this account as an example, select a social situation you have been involved in and do a dramaturgical analysis to describe its context.
2. Provide an illustration of *nonverbal communication* using the story of *Mr. Preedy* as a model.
3. What are some different types of information provided by a *performer* in terms of nonverbal communication which can be used to determine whether or not a person is telling the truth? Provide an illustration.
4. Refer to *Figure 4-1* (p. 82) and using it as a model, diagram your own status and role sets. Identify points of *role conflict* and *role strain*.
5. What are three ways in which language functions to define the sexes differently? Provide an illustration for each.

6. Describe what is going on in the story at the beginning of the chapter regarding Harold and Sybil. Why do you think men tend not to ask for directions?
7. What is *ethnomethodology*?
8. Define the concept *idealization*. Provide an illustration using the doctor's office as a model.
9. Provide an illustration of the *Thomas theorem* from experiences you have had at college.
10. Using the ideas presented in the Global Sociology Box "Emotions in Global Perspective: Do People Everywhere Feel the Same", what illustration from your own personal experience can you give in which your emotions were inconsistent with those from another culture. What contradictory norms caused this inconsistency?
11. What are the basic characteristics of *humour*? Write out a joke and analyze how it manifests the characteristics discussed in the text.

PART VI: ANSWERS TO STUDY QUESTIONS

True-False

1. F (p. 80)
2. F (p. 80)
3. F (p. 80)
4. F (p. 80)
5. T (p. 82)
6. T (p. 82)
7. F (p. 84)
8. F (p. 84)
9. T (p. 85)
10. F (p. 87)
11. F (p. 88)
12. T (p. 89)
13. T (p. 90)
14. F (p. 92)
15. T (p. 92)
16. T (p. 94)
17. T (p. 97)
18. T (pp. 97-98)

Multiple Choice

1. b (p. 79)
2. c (p. 80)
3. d (p. 80)
4. c (pp. 80-81)
5. b (p. 81)
6. d (p. 81)
7. a (p. 81)
8. a (p. 81)
9. a (p. 82)
10. d (p. 82)
11. b (p. 84)
12. e (p. 84)
13. c (p. 85)
14. d (p. 85)
15. b (p. 87)
16. e (p. 87)
17. c (p. 88)
18. a (p. 88)
19. a (p. 89)
20. b (pp. 90-91)
21. d (p. 92)
22. d (p. 93)
23. a (p. 94)
24. c (p. 95)
25. e (pp. 94-97)
26. b (p. 97)

Matching

1. f (p. 81)
2. j (p. 82)
3. a (p. 80)
4. e (p. 79)
5. b (p. 85)
6. i (p. 87)
7. g (p. 89)
8. c (p. 84)
9. h (p. 80)
10. d (p. 82)

Fill-in-the-blank

1. social interaction (p. 79)
2. status, role (pp. 80-81)
3. ascribed (p. 80)
4. role conflict (p. 82)
5. Thomas theorem (p. 84)
6. ethnomethodology (p. 85)
7. dramaturgical (p. 87)
8. presentation of self (p. 87)
9. back (p. 87)

10. anger, fear, happiness, disgust, surprise, sadness (p. 88)
11. demeanor (p. 89)
12. idealization (pp. 90-91)
13. control, value, attention (p. 93)
14. intends, hears (p. 95)
15. conventional, unconventional (p. 94)

PART VII: IN FOCUS—MAJOR ISSUES

1. Define and illustrate the following components of *social structure*.

   A. Status

   B. Achieved Status

   C. Ascribed Status

   D. Master Status

   E. Status Set

   F. Role

   G. Role Set

   H. Role Strain

I. Role Conflict

J. Role Exit

2. Define and illustrate the following as each relates to the *social construction of reality*.
    A. The Thomas theorem

    B. Ethnomethodology

3. Discuss *dramaturgical analysis* by illustrating the following concepts—*performances, nonverbal communication, gender and performance, idealization, embarrassment* and *tact*.

4. Illustrate each of the following ways in which *language defines men and women*.
    A. Language and Power

    B. Language and Value

    C. Language and Attention

5. Using a joke or jokes to illustrate, provide evidence for the following:
   A. The *functions of humour*

   B. The *dynamics of humour*

   C. The *topics of humour*

PART VIII: ANALYSIS AND COMMENT

Window on the World – Global Map 4-1
"Housework in Global Perspective"
Key Points: Questions:

Seeing Ourselves – National Map 4-1
"Do you use Alternative Medicine?"
Key Points: Questions:

Global Sociology
"The Sociology of Emotions: Do People Everywhere Feel the Same?"
Key Points: Questions:

Society: The Basics, Second Canadian Edition

Applying Sociology
"Hide Those Lyin' Eyes: Can You Do It?"

Key Points: Questions:

Applying Sociology
"Gender and Language: You Just Don't Understand!"

Key Points: Questions:

Critical Thinking
"Double Take: Real Headlines that Make People Laugh"

Key Points: Questions:

Groups and Organizations

PART I: CHAPTER OUTLINE

1. Social Groups
   A. Primary and Secondary Groups
   B. Group Leadership
   C. Group Conformity
   D. Reference Groups
   E. Ingroups and Outgroups
   F. Group Size
   G. Social Diversity: Race, Class, and Gender
   H. Networks
2. Formal Organizations
   A. Types of Formal Organizations
   B. Origins of Bureaucracy
   C. Characteristics of Bureaucracy
   D. Organizational Environment
   E. The Informal Side of Bureaucracy
   F. Problems of Bureaucracy
3. The Evolution of Formal Organizations
   A. Scientific Management
   B. The First Challenge: Race and Gender
   C. The Second Challenge: The Japanese Organization
   D. The Third Challenge: The Changing Nature of Work
   E. The "McDonaldization" of Society
   F. The Future of Organization: Opposing Trends
4. Summary
5. Key Concepts
6. Critical-Thinking Questions
7. Applications and Exercises
8. Sites to See

Society: The Basics, Second Canadian Edition

PART II: LEARNING OBJECTIVES

1. To be able to identify the differences between primary groups, secondary groups, aggregates, and categories.
2. To be able to identify the various types of leaders associated with social groups.
3. To be able to compare and contrast the research of several different social scientists on group conformity.
4. To be able to recognize the importance of reference groups to group dynamics.
5. To be able to distinguish between ingroups and outgroups.
6. To understand the relevance of group size to the dynamics of social groups.
7. To be able to identify the types of formal organizations.
8. To be able to identify and describe the basic characteristics of bureaucracy.
9. To become aware of both the limitations and informal side of bureaucracy.
10. To be able to consider ways of humanizing bureaucracy.
11. To consider the issue of the McDonaldization of society.
12. To analyse formal organizations from a cross-cultural perspective.

PART III: KEY CONCEPTS

bureaucracy

bureaucratic inertia

bureaucratic ritualism

dyad

expressive leadership

formal organizations

groupthink

ingroup

instrumental leadership

network

oligarchy

organizational environment

outgroup

primary group

rationality

rationalization

Study Guide

reference group

scientific management

secondary group

social group

tradition

triad

PART IV: IMPORTANT RESEARCHERS

Max Weber   Solomon Asch

Georg Simmel   Irving Janis

Charles Horton Cooley   Samuel Stouffer

Amitai Etzioni   Rosabeth Moss Kanter

Stanley Milgram   Robert Michels

Society: The Basics, Second Canadian Edition

William Ouchi			Sally Helgesen

Deborah Tannen			George Ritzer

PART V: STUDY QUESTIONS
True-False

1. T F Any collection of individuals can be called a *group*.
2. T F While members of *categories* could potentially become transformed into a social group, by definition members of *crowds* cannot be transformed into social groups.
3. T F *Secondary groups* tend to be smaller than *primary groups*.
4. T F *Expressive leadership* emphasizes the completion of tasks.
5. T F The *democratic leadership style* is more expressive than the *authoritarian leadership style*.
6. T F *Stanley Milgram's* research on group conformity patterns illustrated that most individuals are sceptical about the legitimacy of authority for people in positions of power.
7. T F *Samuel Stouffer's* research on soldiers' attitudes toward their own promotions during World War II demonstrates the significance of reference groups in making judgments about ourselves.
8. T F According to research by *Georg Simmel*, large groups tend to be more stable than small groups, such as dyads.
9. T F *Networks* tend to be more enduring and provide a greater sense of identity than most other types of social groups.
10. T F *Normative organizations* are defined as those which impose restrictions on people who have been labelled as deviant.
11. T F A voluntary organization is an example of a *utilitarian organization*.
12. T F According to *Max Weber*, diffusion of responsibility is a major element of bureaucratic organizations.
13. T F The *organizational environment* includes economic and political trends.

14. T F *Bureaucratic inertia* refers to a preoccupation with rules and regulations to the point of thwarting an organization's goals.

15. T F According to research by Deborah Tannen, a "female advantage" for organizations is that women have a greater *information focus* than men.

16. T F According to research by William Ouchi, formal organizations in Japan tend to be characterized by greater *holistic involvement* than formal organizations in North America.

17. T F Salary differences between executives and workers is about the same in Canada and Japan.

18. T F A basic organizational principle in the *McDonaldization of society* is efficiency.

Multiple Choice

1. What is the sociological term for all people with a *common status*, such as "college student"?
   a) a crowd
   b) a group
   c) a category
   d) a population
   e) a social organization

2. A temporary cluster of individuals who may or may not interact is referred to as a
   a) population.
   b) group.
   c) category.
   d) crowd.

3. A social group characterized by long-term personal relationships usually involving many activities is a _____.
   a) primary group
   b) secondary group
   c) category
   d) aggregate
   e) normative organization

4. Which of the following is *not* true of *primary groups*?
   a) they provide security for their members
   b) they are focussed around specific activities
   c) they are valued in and of themselves
   d) they are viewed as ends in themselves

5. Which of the following theorists differentiated between *primary* and *secondary* groups?
   a) Max Weber
   b) Amitai Etzioni
   c) Emile Durkheim
   d) Charles Horton Cooley
   e) George Herbert Mead

6. Which of the following is *not* a characteristic of a *secondary group*?
   a) large size
   b) weak emotional ties
   c) personal orientation
   d) variable, often short duration

7. Members of *secondary groups* display what type of orientation?
   a) personal
   b) residual
   c) natural
   d) closed
   e) goal

8. What is the term for a *group leadership* that emphasizes the completion of tasks?
   a) task group leadership
   b) laissez-faire leadership
   c) expressive leadership
   d) instrumental leadership

9. Which of the following is *not* identified in the text as a *leadership style*?
   a) laissez-faire
   b) democratic
   c) authoritarian
   d) utilitarian

10. Which *style of leadership* is least effective in promoting group goals?
    a) instrumental
    b) laissez-faire
    c) authoritarian
    d) democratic

11. What *style of leader* tends to downplay their position and power, allowing the group to function more of less on its own?
    a) authoritarian
    b) democratic
    c) laissez-faire
    d) bureaucratic
    e) instrumental

12. Crisis situations in social groups are most likely to be quickly resolved when the *leader* is
    a) affective.
    b) laissez-faire.
    c) authoritarian.
    d) democratic.

13. Solomon Asch's classic investigation of group dynamics revealed the dramatic effects of
    a) leadership styles.
    b) leadership types.
    c) primary groups.
    d) group conformity.

14. Which researcher concluded that people are not likely to question authority figures even common sense dictates that they should?
    a) Solomon Asch
    b) Irving Janis
    c) Stanley Milgram
    d) Charles Horton Cooley

15. The November 1998 pepper-spraying of students protesting at the APEC summit is used as an example of
    a) ingroups and outgroups.
    b) reference groups.
    c) bureaucracy.
    d) oligarchy.
    e) groupthink.

16. What is the sociological term for a limited understanding of some issue due to group conformity?
    a) conformist cognizance
    b) groupthink
    c) doublethink
    d) red tape
    e) instrumentalism

17. The term for a social group that serves as a point of reference in making evaluations or decisions is
    a) a control group.
    b) a reference group.
    c) an externalized group.
    d) an internalized group.

18. A social group commanding a member's esteem and loyalty is a(n)
    a) ingroup.
    b) outgroup.
    c) reference group.
    d) subculture.
    e) residual group.

19. Which of the following is *not* one of the ways in which *social diversity* influences inter-group contact?
    a) Large groups turn inward.
    b) Heterogeneous groups turn outward.
    c) Large groups turn outward.
    d) Physical boundaries foster social boundaries.

20. Large secondary groups that are organized to achieve their goals efficiently are referred to as
    a) social organizations.
    b) bureaucracies.
    c) formal organizations.
    d) businesses.

21. *Amitai Etzioni* constructed a typology of *formal organizations*. Organizations such as the CIDA, the Lions Club, and the whites-only organization Stormfront illustrate the type of organization he called
    a) utilitarian
    b) coercive
    c) normative
    d) hierarchal

22. What types of *formal organizations* bestow material benefits on their members?
    a) normative organizations
    b) coercive organizations
    c) social organizations
    d) utilitarian organizations
    e) hierarchal organizations

23. Which of the following is *not* a type of formal organization as identified by *Amitai Etzioni*?
    a) coercive
    b) normative
    c) hierarchal
    d) utilitarian

24. What term refers to an *organizational model* rationally designed to perform complex tasks efficiently?
    a) bureaucracy
    b) complex organization
    c) humanized organization
    d) social organization

25. Which of the following is *not* part of the *organizational environment*?
    a) economic trends
    b) political trends
    c) population patterns
    d) other organizations
    e) company employees

26. *Bureaucratic ritualism* is
    a) the process of promoting people to their level of incompetence.
    b) the tendency of bureaucratic organizations to persist over time.
    c) the rule of the many by the few.
    d) a preoccupation with rules and regulations to the point of thwarting an organization's goals.

27. *Robert Michels* identified one of the limitations of bureaucracy to be the tendency of bureaucracy to become dominated by *oligarchy* because
    a) technical competence cannot be maintained.
    b) hierarchy undermines democracy.
    c) bureaucrats get caught up in rule-making.
    d) specialization gives way to generalist orientations.

28. According to *Rosabeth Moss Kanter's* research
    a) proper application of technology in bureaucracy is critical for success.
    b) oligarchy is effective in bureaucratic structures during times of rapid change.
    c) race and gender issues must be addressed as they relate to organizational hierarchies.
    d) humanizing bureaucracies would diminish productivity.
    e) none of the above.

29. Which of the following is *not* identified by *Sally Helgesen* as a gender-linked issue in organizations?
    a) attentiveness to interconnections
    b) flexibility
    c) worker productivity
    d) communication skills

30. Research by Deborah Tannen on *gender* and management styles has found that men tend to have a(n)
    a) image focus.
    b) information focus.
    c) flexibility focus.
    d) developmental focus.

Matching

1. ____ The tendency of group members to conform by adopting a narrow view of some issue.
2. ____ A social group that serves as a point of reference in making evaluations or decisions.
3. ____ A small social group in which relationships are personal and enduring.
4. ____ Two or more people who identify and interact with one another.
5. ____ People who share a status in common.
6. ____ Group leaders who emphasize the completion of tasks.
7. ____ Large and impersonal groups based on a specific interest or activity.
8. ____ A social group with two members.
9. ____ Large, secondary groups that are organized to achieve their goals efficiently.
10. ____ An organizational model rationally designed to perform complex tasks efficiently.

a. secondary
b. formal organization
c. groupthink
d. instrumental leadership
e. social group
f. reference group
g. dyad
h. bureaucracy
i. primary group
j. category

Fill-in-the-blank

1. A _____ _____ is defined as two or more people who identify and interact with one another.

2. Political organizations, college and university classes are examples of _____ *groups*.

3. While *primary* relationships have a _____ orientation, *secondary* relationships have a _____ orientation.

4. _____ *leadership* refers to group leadership that emphasizes the completion of tasks.

5. _____ *leaders* focus on instrumental concerns, make decisions on their own, and demand strict compliance from subordinates.

6. *Irving Janis* studies the process he called _____ that reduces a group's capacity for critical reflection.

7. A social group that consists of *two* members is known as a _____.

8. Peter Blau points out three ways in which the *social diversity* influences intergroup contact, including large groups turn _____, _____ groups turn outward, and physical boundaries foster _____ boundaries.

9. A _____ is a web of social ties that links people who identify and interact little with one another.

10. Amitai Etzioni has identified three *type of formal organizations*, distinguished by why people participate in them. Ones that pay their members are called _____ organizations. People become members of _____ organizations to pursue goals they consider morally worthwhile. Finally, _____ organizations are distinguished by involuntary membership.

11. A _____ is an organizational model rationally designed to perform complex tasks efficiently.

12. Preoccupation with rules and regulations to the point of thwarting an organization's goals is called *bureaucratic* _____.

13. *Bureaucratic* _____ is the term used to describe the tendency of bureaucratic organizations to perpetuate themselves.

14. The *organizational environment* includes several dimensions, including _____, _____ and _____ *trends*, _____ *patterns*, and *other* _____.

15. *Deborah Tannen's* research on management styles suggests that women have a greater _____ *focus* and men have greater _____ focus.

16. The five basic principles of *Japanese organizations* are _____ and _____, *lifetime* _____, _____ involvement, broad-based _____, and _____ decision-making.

17. Four ways in which today's organizations are different than a century ago are: they allow for greater _____, there is more emphasis on _____ work teams, there is a _____ organizational structure, and greater _____.

18. The four characteristics of the *McDonaldization of society* include _____, _____, _____ and _____, and _____ through *automation*.

19. Nona Glaser sees the clerkless customer as an _____ worker.

20. While the post-industrial economy has produced many highly skilled jobs, the number of routine service jobs has _____ dramatically.

Definition and Short-Answer

1. Differentiate between the qualities of *bureaucracies* and *small groups*. In what ways are they similar?
2. What is the relationship between groups discussions and *groupthink*?
3. What are three major *limitations* of bureaucracy? Define and provide an illustration for each.
4. In what ways do bureaucratic organizations in *Japan* differ from those in Canada? What are the consequences of these differences? Relate this comparison to the issue of *humanizing* organizations.
5. Differentiate between the concepts of *group* and *category*.

Society: The Basics, Second Canadian Edition

6. Identify the basic *types of leadership* in groups and provide examples of the relative advantages and disadvantage for each type.
7. What are the general characteristics of the *McDonaldization* of society? Provide an illustration of this phenomenon in our society based on your own experience.
8. What are the some paths to *humanizing organizations*? How does the research of Rosabeth Kanter relate to this issue?
9. What are Peter Blau's points concerning how the structure of social groups regulates intergroup association?
10. What are the three *types of organizations* identified by Amitai Etzioni? Describe and provide an illustration for each.

PART VI: ANSWERS TO STUDY QUESTIONS

True-False
1. F (p. 101)
2. F (p. 102)
3. F (p. 102)
4. F (p. 103)
5. T (p. 104)
6. F (pp.104-105)
7. T (p. 106)
8. T (p. 107)
9. F (p. 109)
10. F (p. 110)
11. F (p. 110)
12. T (p. 112)
13. T (p. 113)
14. F (p. 114)
15. T (p. 117)
16. T (p. 118)
17. F (p. 118)
18. T (p. 120)

Multiple Choice
1. c (pp.100-102)
2. d (p. 102)
3. a (p. 102)
4. b (p. 102)
5. d (p. 102)
6. c (p. 102)
7. e (p. 103)
8. d (p. 103)
9. d (p. 104)
10. b (p. 104)
11. c (p. 104)
12. c (p. 104)
13. d (p. 104)
14. c (pp.104-105)
15. e (p. 105)
16. b (p. 105)
17. b (p. 105)
18. a (p. 106)
19. c (pp.107-108)
20. c (p. 110)
21. c (p. 110)
22. d (p. 110)
23. c (p. 110)
24. a (p. 111)
25. e (p. 113)
26. d (p. 114)
27. b (p. 115)
28. c (p. 117)
29. c (p. 117)
30. a (p. 117)

Matching
1. c (p. 105)
2. f (p. 105)
3. i (p. 101)
4. e (p. 101)
5. j (pp.101-102)
6. d (p. 103)
7. a (p. 102)
8. g (p. 107)
9. b (p. 110)
10. h (p. 111)

Fill-in-the-blank
1. social group (p. 101)
2. secondary (p. 102)
3. personal, goal (p. 103)
4. instrumental (p. 103)
5. authoritarian (p. 114)
6. groupthink (p. 105)
7. dyad (p. 107)
8. inward, heterogeneous, social (pp. 101-108)
9. network (p. 109)
10. utilitarian, normative, coercive (p. 110)
11. bureaucracy (p. 111)
12. ritualism (p. 114)

13. inertia (p. 114)
14. technological, economic, political, population, organizations (p. 113)
15. information, image (p. 117)
16. hiring, advancement, security, holistic, training, collective (p. 118)
17. autonomy, competitive, flatter, flexibility (p. 119)
18. efficiency, calculability, uniformity, predictability, control (pp. 120-121)
19. unpaid (p. 122)
20. increased (p. 121)

PART VII: IN FOCUS—MAJOR ISSUES
1. Identify the major characteristics of the following *types of group*.
    A. primary group

    B. secondary group

2. Differentiate between the following *types of leadership*.
    A. instrumental leadership

    B. expressive leadership

3. Differentiate between the following *styles of leadership*.
    A. authoritarian leadership

    B. democratic leadership

    C. laissez-faire leadership

4. Define and illustrate the following *types of formal organizations*.
   A. normative

   B. coercive

   C. utilitarian

5. Identify and define the six *elements of the ideal bureaucratic organization*.

6. Define and illustrate the following *problems of bureaucracy*.
   A. bureaucratic alienation

   B. bureaucratic inertia

   C. oligarchy

7. Define the term *scientific management*.

8. Identify and describe or illustrate the four ways organizations today differ from those of a century ago.

9. Identify five major distinctions between formal organizations in Japan and Canada.

10. Identify and illustrate the *four basic principles* of the *"McDonaldization of society."*

Society: The Basics, Second Canadian Edition

PART VIII: ANALYSIS AND COMMENT

Window on the World – Global Map 5-1
"High Technology in Global Perspective"
Key Points: Questions:

Global Sociology
"The Internet: A Global Network"
Key Points: Questions:

Applying Sociology
"The 'Spin' Game: Choosing Our Words Carefully"
Key Points: Questions:

Critical Thinking
"Is More Efficient and Convenient Always Better?"
Key Points: Questions:

Deviance

PART I: CHAPTER OUTLINE
1. What is Deviance?
    A. The Biological Context
    B. Personality Factors
    C. The Social Foundations of Deviance
2. The Functions of Deviance: Structural-Functional Analysis
    A. Durkheim's Basic Insight
    B. Merton's Strain Theory
    C. Deviant Subcultures
3. Labelling Deviance: The Symbolic-Interaction Approach
    A. Labelling Theory
    B. Primary and Secondary Deviance
    C. Stigma
    D. Labelling and Mental Illness
    E. The Medicalization of Deviance
    F. Sutherland's Differential Association Theory
    G. Hirschi's Control Theory
4. Deviance and Inequality: Social Conflict Analysis
    A. Deviance and Power
    B. Deviance and Capitalism
    C. White-Collar Crime
    D. Corporate Crime
    E. Organized Crime
5. Deviance and Social Diversity
    A. Hate crimes
    B. Deviance and Gender
6. Crime
    A. Types of Crime
    B. Criminal Statistics
    C. The "Street" Criminal: A Profile
    D. Crime in Global Perspective

7. The Criminal Justice System
   A. Police
   B. Courts
   C. Punishment
8. Summary
9. Key Concepts
10. Critical-Thinking Questions
11. Applications and Exercises
12. Sites to See

PART II: LEARNING OBJECTIVES
1. To be able to explain how deviance is interpreted as a product of society.
2. To be able to identify and evaluate the biological explanation of deviance.
3. To be able to identify and evaluate the psychological explanation of deviance.
4. To be able to identify and evaluate the sociological explanations of deviance.
5. To be able to compare and contrast different theories representative of the three major sociological paradigms.
6. To be able to evaluate empirical evidence used to support these different sociological theories of deviance.
7. To be able to distinguish among the types of crime.
8. To become more aware of the demographic patterns of crime in our society.
9. To evaluate deviance in global context.
10. To be able to identify and describe the elements of our criminal justice system.

PART III: KEY CONCEPTS

clearance rates

corporate crime

crime

crimes against property

crimes against the person

criminal justice system

criminal recidivism

deterrence

deviance

hate crime

labelling theory

medicalization of deviance

organized crime

plea bargaining

rehabilitation

retribution

social control

social protection

stigma

white-collar crime

victimless crime

PART IV: IMPORTANT RESEARCHERS

Caesare Lombroso	Albert Cohen and Walter Miller
William Sheldon	Walter Reckless and Simon Dintz
Steven Spitzer	Edwin Sutherland
Richard Cloward and Lloyd Ohlin	Thomas Szasz

Society: The Basics, Second Canadian Edition

Emile Durkheim   Howard Becker

Robert Merton   Erving Goffman

Travis Hirschi

PART V: STUDY QUESTIONS

True-False

1. T F   Using the sociological perspective, *social control* is broadly understood, including the criminal justice system as well as the general socialization process.
2. T F   What deviant actions have in common is some element of *difference*.
3. T F   Research cited in the text clearly concludes there is absolutely no relationship between *biology* and crime.
4. T F   *Containment theory* focuses our attention on how certain behaviours are linked to, or contained by, our genes.
5. T F   One of the *social foundations of deviance* is that deviance varies according to cultural norms.
6. T F   According to Emile Durkheim, deviance affirms cultural values and norms.
7. T F   In Robert Merton's *strain theory* the concept deviance is applied by linking deviance to certain social imbalances between *goals* and *means*.
8. T F   Walter Miller's *subcultural theory* of deviance points out that deviant subcultures have *no focal concerns*, and therefore have no social norms to guide the behaviour of their members.
9. T F   *Primary deviance* tends to be more harmful to society than *secondary deviance*.
10. T F Thomas Szasz argues that *mental illness* is a *myth* and is a label used by the powerful in society to force people to follow dominant cultural norms.

11. T F Our authors suggest that during the last fifty years there has been a trend away from what is known as the *medicalization of deviance*.
12. T F Edwin Sutherland's *differential association theory* suggests that certain individuals are incapable of learning from experience and therefore are more likely to become deviant.
13. T F Travis Hirschi's *control theory* states that social control depends on anticipating consequences of one's behaviour.
14. T F The *social-conflict* perspective links deviance to social inequality and power in society.
15. T F *White-collar crime* is defined as crime committed by people of high social position in the course of their occupations.
16. T F While *civil law* regulates business dealings between private parties, *criminal law* defines the individual's moral responsibilities to society.
17. T F What qualifies an offense as a *hate crime* is not so much a matter of the race or ancestry of the victim as it is the *motivation* of the offender.
18. T F Virtually every society in the world applies more stringent normative controls on *men* than to *women*.
19. T F According to the Uniform Crime Reporting (UCR) survey, robbery and murder are examples of *crimes against the person*.
20. T F Comparisons with *victimization surveys* show that the official crime statistics are a good estimate of the crime rate.
21. T F *Plea Bargaining* gives everybody a fair chance of presenting their side of the story.
22. T F Studies show that those with longer sentences have lower rates of *Criminal recidivism*.

Multiple Choice

1. _____ refers to the recognized violation of cultural norms.
   a) Crime
   b) Deviance
   c) Residual behaviour
   d) Social control
   e) Law

2. *Containment theory* is an example of a(n) _____ explanation of deviance.
   a) biological
   b) psychological
   c) anthropological
   d) sociological

3. Which of the following is *not a social foundation* of deviance?
   a) Deviance varies according to cultural norms.
   b) People become deviant in that others define them that way.
   c) Both norms and the way people define social situations involve social power.
   d) All are identified as foundations of deviance.

Society: The Basics, Second Canadian Edition

4. *Emile Durkheim* theorized that all but which of the following are *functions of deviance*?
   a) It clarifies moral boundaries.
   b) It affirms cultural values and norms.
   c) It encourages social stability.
   d) It promotes social unity.

5. Which of the following theories is derived from the *structural-functional paradigm*?
   a) strain theory
   b) labelling theory
   c) differential association theory
   d) control theory

6. *Robert Merton's strain theory* is a component of which broad theoretical paradigm?
   a) social-conflict
   b) structural-functional
   c) symbolic-interactionism
   d) social-exchange
   e) human ecology

7. According to Robert Merton's *strain theory*, one response to the inability to succeed is _____, or the rejection of both cultural goals and means—so one, in effect, "drops out."
   a) innovation
   b) inertia
   c) ritualism
   d) retreatism

8. Which of the following is *not* an example of a *deviant subculture* identified in *Richard Cloward* and *Lloyd Olhin's* research on delinquents?
   a) residual
   b) criminal
   c) retreatist
   d) conflict

9. Which of the following is an appropriate criticism of *structural-functional theories* of deviance?
   a) The theories assume a diversity of cultural standards.
   b) The theories assume a single cultural standard.
   c) The theories imply that everyone who breaks the rules will be labelled deviant.
   d) The theories overplay the importance of societal definitions of deviance.

10. Which theory asserts that deviance and conformity result from the responses of others?
    a) differential association
    b) social conflict
    c) labelling
    d) structural-functionalism

11. Skipping school for the first time as an eighth grader is an example of
    a) recidivism.
    b) primary deviance.
    c) a degradation ceremony.
    d) secondary deviance.

12. What is Erving Goffman's term for a powerful negative social label that radically changes a person's self-concept and social identity?
    a) anomie
    b) secondary deviance
    c) medicalization of deviance
    d) retribution
    e) stigma

13. Sometimes an entire community formally stigmatizes an individual through what *Harold Garfinkel* called a
    a) hate crime.
    b) retrospective label.
    c) recidivism process.
    d) degradation ceremony.
    e) conflict subculture.

14. Once people stigmatize an individual, they may engage in _____, or interpreting someone's past in light of some present deviance.
    a) retrospective labelling
    b) projective labelling
    c) residual labelling
    d) ad hoc labelling
    e) labelling inertia

15. What is the *medicalization of deviance*?
    a) the recognition of the true source of deviance
    b) the objective, clinical approach to deviant behaviour
    c) the transformation of moral and legal issues into medical models
    d) the discovery of the links between biochemical properties and deviance

16. *Attachment, involvement, commitment,* and *belief* are all types of social control in
    a) Sutherland's differential association theory.
    b) Durkheim's functional theory.
    c) Goffman's labelling theory.
    d) Cohen's subcultural theory.
    e) Hirschi's control theory.

17. According to the *social-conflict paradigm*, who and what is labelled deviant is based primarily on:
    a) the severity of the deviant act.
    b) psychological profile.
    c) the functions being served.
    d) relative power.

18. What is the term for crime committed by persons of high social position in the course of their occupations?
    a) occupational crimes
    b) status offenses
    c) white-collar crime
    d) residual crime

19. _____ defines the individual's moral responsibility to society.
    a) Civil law
    b) Criminal law
    c) Medicalization
    d) Stigma
    e) Attachment

20. _____ *crime* is a business supplying illegal goods or services.
    a) Victimless
    b) Residual
    c) Corporate
    d) Organized
    e) Structural

21. Which of the following are criticisms of *social-conflict theory*?
    a) It is an oversimplification to imply that all the laws and other cultural norms are created directly by the rich and powerful.
    b) It implies that criminality springs up only to the extent that a society treats its members unequally.
    c) Both (a) and (b) is a criticism of social-conflict theory.
    d) Neither (a) nor (b) are criticisms of social conflict theory.

22. Consider these statements: "While what is deviant may vary, deviance itself is found in all societies." "Deviance and the social response it provokes serve to maintain the moral foundation of society." "Deviance can direct social change." All help to summarize which sociological explanation of deviance?
    a) social-conflict
    b) structural-functional
    c) symbolic-interaction
    d) labelling
    e) social exchange

23. Which contribution below is attributed to the *structural-functional theory* of deviance?
    a) Nothing is inherently deviant.
    b) The reactions of others to deviance are highly variable.
    c) Deviance is found in all societies.
    d) Laws and other norms reflect the interests of the powerful in society.

24. Your authors suggest that another way to look at _____ is to say that people who commit such crimes are themselves both offenders and victims.
    a) crimes against the person
    b) crimes against property
    c) traffic offences
    d) victimless crimes

25. Which of the following is *not* a type of *victimless crime*?
    a) gambling
    b) prostitution
    c) arson
    d) illegal drug use

26. In the case of *property crimes*, 78 percent of the people arrested are men. For *violent crimes*, of all those arrested, ___ percent are men.
    a) 46
    b) 52
    c) 73
    d) 86

27. The United States' *homicide rate* is ___ the rate in Canada.
    a) about the same as
    b) twice as high as
    c) about three times higher than
    d) more than three times higher than

28. Which of the following is *not listed* as a *justification for punishment* in our criminal justice system?
    a) retribution
    b) societal protection
    c) deterrence
    d) rehabilitation
    e) all of the above are justifications

29. Which of the following countries has the highest incarceration rate?
    a) Belize
    b) United States
    c) Kazakhstan
    d) Russia
    e) Bahamas

30. About _____ percent of those convicted of a Criminal Code offence are convicted of a new offence within three years.
    a) 20
    b) 35
    c) 50
    d) 65
    e) 80

31. Some studies suggest that almost _____ out of five offenders are eventually convicted again.
    a) 1
    b) 2
    c) 3
    d) 4
    e) 5

Society: The Basics, Second Canadian Edition

Matching

1. ____ According to Robert Merton's *strain theory*, these are different ways of responding to the inability to succeed through conformity.
2. ____ The assertion that deviance and conformity result, not so much from what people do, as from how others respond to those actions.
3. ____ Violations of law in which there are no apparent victims.
4. ____ Types of *social controls* according to Travis Hirschi.
5. ____ Crime in the *suites*.
6. ____ Types of *deviant subcultures* identified by Richard Cloward and Lloyd Ohlin's theory of relative opportunity structure.
7. ____ A legal negotiation in which the prosecution reduces a charge in exchange for a defendant's guilty plea.
8. ____ The recognized violation of cultural norms.
9. ____ Attempts by society to regulate people's thought and behaviour.
10. ____ A powerfully negative label that radically changes a person's self-concept and social identity.

a. criminal, conflict, retreatist
b. victimless crime
c. plea bargaining
d. labelling theory
e. attachment, involvement, belief, commitment
f. deviance
g. stigma
h. social control
i. retreatism, rebellion, ritualism, innovation
j. white collar crime

Fill-in-the-blank

1. _____ is the violation of norms a society formally enacts into criminal law.

2. The _____ _____ _____ is the formal response to alleged violations of law on the part of police, courts, and prison officials.

3. *William Sheldon* argued that _____ _____ might predict criminality.

4. A *psychological explanation* of deviance that posits the view that if boys have developed strong moral values and a positive self-image they will not become delinquents is called _____ theory.

5. The *social foundations of deviance* include: Deviance varies according to _____ _____; People become deviant as others _____ them that way; And, both norms and the way people define situations involve social _____.

6. The *strain theory* of deviance is based on the _____-_____ *paradigm*.

7. *Richard Cloward* and *Lloyd Ohlin* explain deviance and conformity in terms of the _____ _____ structure young people face in their lives.

8. Activity that is initially defined as deviant is called _____ *deviance*. On the other hand, a person who accepts the label of deviant may then engage in _____ *deviance*, or behaviour caused by the person's incorporating the deviant label into their self-concept.

9. Psychiatrist Thomas Szasz argues that *mental illness* is a _____.

10. Travis Hirschi links *conformity* to four types of social control, including _____, _____, _____, and _____.

11. *Social-conflict theory* demonstrates that deviance reflects *social* _____. This approach suggests that *who* or *what* is labelled as deviant is based largely on the relative _____ of categories of people.

12. _____-_____ *crime* is defined as crimes committed by persons of high social position in the course of their occupations.

13. _____ *law* refers to general regulations involving economic affairs between private parties.

14. _____ *surveys* show that the actual level of crime is three times as great as that indicated by official reports.

15. The *criminal justice system* in Canada consists of three elements: _____, _____, and _____.

16. The four basic *justifications for punishment* include: _____, _____, _____, and _____ _____.

17. Subsequent offenses by people previously convicted of crimes is termed *criminal* _____.

18. Since the early 1990s there has been a slight _____ in the number of admissions to Canadian jails.

Definition and Short-Answer

1. According to *Travis Hirschi's control theory* there are four types of social controls. What are these? Provide an example of each.
2. According to *Robert Merton's strain theory*, what are the four deviant responses by individuals to dominant cultural patterns when there is a gap between *means* and *goals*? Provide an illustration of each.
3. According to *Emile Durkheim*, what are the *functions of deviance*? Provide an illustration for each.
4. *Social-conflict* theorist *Steven Spitzer* argues that deviant labels are applied to people who impede the operation of *capitalism*. What are the four reasons he gives for this phenomenon?
5. How do researchers using *differential association theory* explain deviance?
6. What is meant by the term *medicalization of deviance*? Provide two illustrations.
7. Outline the evidence for and against the argument that widely different gun laws explain why the homicide rate is so much lower in Canada than in the United States.
8. What are the four *justifications* for the use of punishment against criminals? What evidence exists for their relative effectiveness?
9. *Richard Cloward* and *Lloyd Ohlin* investigated delinquent youth and explain deviance and conformity in terms of the *relative opportunity structure* young people face in their lives. Identify and define the three types of *subcultures* these researchers have identified as representing the criminal lifestyles of delinquent youth.
10. Describe *Thomas Szasz's* view of mental illness and deviance. What is your opinion of his arguments?
11. Briefly review the demographic *profile* of the *street criminal*.
12. Critique the official statistics of crime in Canada. What are the weaknesses of the measures used in the identification of *crime rates*?
13. What are the three consequences for the deviant person depending on whether a *moral model* or *medical model* is applied?

PART VI: ANSWERS TO STUDY QUESTIONS

True-False
1. T (p. 128)
2. T (p. 128)
3. F (p. 128)
4. F (p. 129)
5. T (p. 129)
6. T (p. 130)
7. T (p. 130)
8. F (p. 131)
9. F (p. 133)
10. T (p. 134)
11. F (p. 134)
12. F (p. 135)
13. T (p. 135)
14. T (p. 136)
15. T (p. 137)
16. T (p. 138)
17. T (p. 139)
18. F (p. 139)
19. T (p. 140)
20. F (p. 140)
21. F (p. 145)
22. F (p. 148)

Multiple Choice
1. b (p. 128)
2. b (p. 129)
3. d (p. 129)
4. c (p. 130)
5. a (p. 130)
6. b (p. 130)
7. d (p. 131)
8. a (p. 131)
9. b (p. 132)
10. c (p. 132)
11. b (p. 133)
12. e (p. 133)
13. d (p. 134)
14. a (p. 134)
15. c (p. 134)
16. e (pp.135-136)
17. d (p. 136)
18. c (p. 137)
19. b (p. 138)
20. d (p. 138)
21. c (p. 139)
22. b (p. 139)
23. c (p. 138)
24. d (p. 140)
25. c (p. 140)
26. c (p. 142)
27. d (p. 143)
28. e (p. 147)
29. b (p. 147)
30. c (p. 148)
31. d (p. 148)

Matching
1. i (p. 131)
2. d (p. 132)
3. b (p. 140)
4. e (pp.135-136)
5. j (p. 138)
6. a (p. 131)
7. c (p. 145)
8. f (p. 128)
9. h (p. 128)
10. g (p. 133)

Fill-in-the-blank
1. Crime (p. 128)
2. criminal justice system (p. 128)
3. body structure (p. 128)
4. containment (p. 129)
5. cultural norms, define, power (pp. 129-130)
6. structural-functional (p. 130)
7. relative opportunity (p. 131)
8. primary, secondary (p. 133)
9. myth (p. 134)
10. attachment, commitment, involvement, belief (pp. 136-136)
11. inequality, power (p. 136)
12. white-collar (p. 137)
13. civil (p. 138)
14. victimization (p. 140)
15. police, courts, punishment (p. 145)
16. retribution, deterrence, rehabilitation, societal protection (pp. 146-147)
17. recidivism (p. 147)
18. decrease (p. 147)

Society: The Basics, Second Canadian Edition

PART VII: IN FOCUS—MAJOR ISSUES

1. Emile Durkheim suggested deviance performs four essential *functions*. What are these? Provide an illustration for each.

2. Robert Merton argued that excessive deviance arises from particular social arrangements. What is his theory called? What does his theory tell us about the relationship between *means* and *goals* in society?

3. Walter Miller suggests that *deviant subcultures* are characterized by:

4. Provide an example for each of the *responses to strain* identified in Merton's theory.
    A. conformity

B. innovation

C. ritualism

D. retreatist

E. rebellion

5. Identify the major concepts and ideas related each of the following theories associated with the *symbolic-interaction approach*.
    A. Labelling theory

    B. Differential association theory

    C. Control theory

6. The *social-conflict approach* links deviance to social inequality. What do proponents of this approach suggest about the following?
   A. Deviance and power

   B. Deviance and capitalism

7. What do the government crime reports tell us about the following demographic characteristics of people arrested for *violent* and *property* crime?
   A. Age

   B. Gender

   C. Social class

   D. Race and ethnicity

8. Describe each of the following *components of the criminal justice system.*
   A. Police

B. Courts

C. Punishment

9. Define each of the following four *justifications for punishment*.
   A. Retribution

   B. Deterrence

   C. Rehabilitation

   D. Societal Protection

PART VIII: ANALYSIS AND COMMENT

Global Sociology
"Cockfighting: Cultural Ritual or Abuse of Animals?"
Key Points: Questions:

Society: The Basics, Second Canadian Edition

Window on the World – Global Map 6-1
"Capital Punishment in Global Perspectives"

Key Points: Questions:

Applying Sociology
"Soft on Crime?"

Key Points: Questions:

Sexuality

PART I: CHAPTER OUTLINE
1. Understanding Sexuality
    A. Sex: A Biological Issue
    B. Sex and the Body
    C. Sex: A Cultural Issue
    D. The Incest Taboo
2. Sexual Attitudes In Canada
    A. The Sexual Revolution
    B. The Sexual Counterrevolution
    C. Premarital Sex
    D. Sex Among Adults
    E. Extramarital Sex
3. Sexual Orientation
    A. What Gives Us A Sexual Orientation?
    B. How Many Gay People?
    C. The Gay Rights Movement
4. Sexual Controversies
    A. Teen Pregnancy
    B. Pornography
    C. Prostitution
    D. Sexual Violence and Abuse
5. Theoretical Analysis of Sexuality
    A. Structural-Functional Analysis
    B. Symbolic-Interaction Analysis
    C. Social-Conflict Analysis
6. Summary
7. Key Concepts
8. Critical-Thinking Questions
9. Applications and Exercises
10. Sites to See

PART II: LEARNING OBJECTIVES
1. To gain a sociological understanding of human sexuality focussing on both biological and cultural factors.
2. To become more aware of the sexual attitudes found in Canada today.
3. To be able to describe both the sexual revolution and sexual counter-revolution that occurred during the last half century in Canada.
4. To be able to discuss human sexuality as it is experienced across different stages of the human life course.
5. To be able to discuss issues relating to the biological and social causes of sexual orientation.
6. To be able to describe the demographics of sexual orientation in our society, including the research methods used to obtain such information about our population.
7. To gain a sociological perspective on several sexual controversies, including teen pregnancy, pornography, prostitution, and sexual violence and abuse.
8. To be able to discuss issues relating to human sexuality from the viewpoints offered by structural-functional, symbolic-interactionist, and social-conflict analyses.

PART III: KEY CONCEPTS

abortion

asexuality

bisexuality

heterosexuality

heterosexism

homophobia

homosexuality

incest taboo

intersexed person

pornography

primary sex characteristics

prostitution

queer theory

secondary sex characteristics

sex

sexual orientation

transsexuals

PART IV: IMPORTANT RESEARCHERS
Alfred Kinsey   Simon LeVay

Helen Colton   Kingsley Davis

PART V: STUDY QUESTIONS

True-False

1. T F Social scientists long considered sex *off limits* for research. It was not until the middle of the twentieth century that researchers turned attention to this pervasive dimension of social life.
2. T F In *fertilization*, the male contributes either an X or Y chromosome.
3. T F *Primary sex characteristics* are those that develop during puberty.
4. T F *Intersexed people* feel they are one sex even though biologically they are of the other.
5. T F Sexuality has a *biological* foundation.
6. T F Almost any *sexual practice* shows considerable variation from one society to another.
7. T F Every known culture has some form of *incest taboo*—it is a cultural universal.
8. T F Efforts to regulate sex stopped prior to World War II.
9. T F According to the authors, the *sexual counterrevolution* occurred in our society during the 1960s.
10. T F During this century, attitudes towards *premarital sexual behaviour* has changed more dramatically among females than it has for males.
11. T F According to research data cited in the text, less than half of Canadian teenagers are sexually active.

Society: The Basics, Second Canadian Edition

12. T F Research data suggest that married people have sex more frequently than single people.
13. T F *Sexual orientation* refers to the biological distinction of being female or male.
14. T F Most research indicates that among *homosexuals*, lesbians outnumber gays by a ratio of about two-to-one.
15. T F *Pornography* refers to sexually explicit material that causes sexual arousal.
16. T F Around the world, *prostitution* is greatest in low-income countries where patriarchy is strong and traditional cultural norms limit women's ability to make a living.
17. T F Among sex workers, call girls have the lowest status.
18. T F A common myth is that most victims of *rapes* are raped by strangers.
19. T F Most societies condemn married people for having sex with someone other than their spouse.
20. T F According to national survey research, over fifty percent of adults in Canada think that a woman should be able to obtain a legal *abortion* for any reason if "agreed upon by woman and physician."

Multiple-Choice

1. _____ refers to the biological distinction between females and males.
   a) Gender
   b) Sex
   c) Sexual orientation
   d) Human sexuality

2. In reproduction, a female ovum and a male sperm, each containing _____ chromosomes, combine to form a fertilized embryo. One of these chromosome pairs determines the child's sex.
   a) 12
   b) 7
   c) 23
   d) 31
   e) 48

3. _____ are people who feel they are one sex even though biologically they are of the other sex.
   a) Intersexed person
   b) Transvestites
   c) Homophobics
   d) Transsexuals

4. If an Islamic woman is disturbed by another person while she is bathing, what body part is she most likely to cover?
   a) her feet
   b) her breasts
   c) her navel
   d) her genitals
   e) her face

5. All Canadians who engaged in anal intercourse before _____ committed a crime.
   a) 1929
   b) 1949
   c) 1969
   d) 1989

6. Who said: "[T]he state has no business in the bedrooms of the nation"?
   a) Jean Chrétien
   b) Marilyn Monroe
   c) Alfred Kinsey
   d) Pierre Elliot Trudeau

7. According to the _____, society allows (and even encourages) men to be sexually active, while expecting women to remain chaste before marriage and faithful to their husbands afterwards.
   a) sexual counterrevolution
   b) sexual revolution
   c) double-standard
   d) permissiveness index

8. Approximately ____ *percent* of Canadian adults believe that it is more acceptable to have an affair today than it was ten years ago.
   a) 10
   b) 20
   c) 30
   d) 40
   e) 50

9. _____ refers to a person's preference in terms of sexual partner: same sex, other sex, either sex, neither sex.
   a) Sexual orientation
   b) Sex
   c) Gender
   d) Sexual response

10. Which of the following is a conclusion of the *Kinsey studies*?
    a) The sexual response cycle for women includes eight stages, while for men there is a four stage sexual response cycle.
    b) Homosexuality and heterosexuality are not mutually exclusive categories, but rather exist on a continuum.
    c) Sexual orientation changes two or three times for the average person over his or her lifetime.
    d) none of the above

11. On the issue of adoptions by gays and lesbians, people living in _____ show the highest level of support (55 percent) whereas people living in _____ show the lowest level of support (33 percent.
    a) British Columbia/the Atlantic provinces
    b) Ontario/ Quebec
    c) British Columbia/Ontario
    d) Manitoba and Saskatchewan/Alberta
    e) Quebec/Alberta

12. Which of the following is accurate concerning *teen pregnancy* in Canada?
    a) Approximately 40 000 teens become pregnant each year.
    b) Most teens who get pregnant did not intend to.
    c) Teens who become pregnant are at great risk of poverty.
    d) Canada has a moderately high rate of teen pregnancy compared to that in other high-income societies.
    e) All of the above are accurate.

13. Which of the following is correct about the law on prostitution in Canada?
    a) It is illegal to buy sex.
    b) It is illegal to sell sex.
    c) It is illegal to communicate in private about trading sex.
    d) It is illegal to communicate in public about trading sex.
    e) All of the above correct.

14. Which of the following is *inaccurate* about *prostitution*?
    a) Most prostitutes are women.
    b) Most prostitutes offer heterosexual services.
    c) Call girls are the lowest prestige type of prostitution.
    d) Prostitution is greatest in low-income countries where patriarchy is strong and traditional cultural norms limit women's ability to earn a living.

15. *Prostitution* is classified as being what type of crime?
    a) property
    b) victimless
    c) white-collar
    d) violent

16. Official sexual assault statistics indicate that approximately _____ percent of rape victims are *male*.
    a) 10
    b) 15
    c) less than 2
    d) 21

17. Which of the following is/are evidence of a societal need to *regulate* sex?
    a) Most societies condemn married people for having sex with someone other than their spouse.
    b) Every society has some form of incest taboo.
    c) Historically, the social control of sexuality was strong, mostly because sex commonly led to childbirth.
    d) all of the above

18. _____ refers to a view stigmatizing anyone who is not heterosexual as "queer."
    a) Asexuality
    b) Heterosexism
    c) Bisexuality
    d) Homophobia

19. Which of the following is a criticism of the *symbolic-interactionist paradigm*?
    a) It fails to take into account how social patterns regarding sexuality are socially constructed.
    b) It fails to help us appreciate the variety of sexual practices found over the course of history and around the world.
    c) It fails to identify the broader social structures that establish certain patterns of sexual behaviours cross-culturally.
    d) None of the above are criticisms of symbolic-interactionism.

20. Which of the following is *inaccurate* concerning the sociological perspective offered by the *structural-functionalist paradigm*?
    a) It helps us to appreciate how sexuality plays an important part in how society is organized.
    b) It focuses attention on how societies, through the incest taboo and other cultural norms, have always paid attention to who has sex with who, especially who reproduces with whom.
    c) This approach pays considerable attention to the great diversity of sexual ideas and practices found around the world.
    d) All of the above are accurate.

Matching

1. _____ The biological distinction between females and males.
2. _____ The genitals, organs used for reproduction.
3. _____ A human being with some combination of female and male genitalia.
4. _____ People who feel they are one sex even though biologically they are of the other.
5. _____ Refers to a person's preference in terms of sexual partners.
6. _____ Sexual attraction to someone of the same sex.
7. _____ No sexual attraction to people of either sex.
8. _____ Sexual attraction to people of both sexes.
9. _____ Refers to sexually explicit material that causes sexual arousal.
10. _____ The selling of sexual services.
11. _____ A view stigmatizing anyone who is not heterosexual as "queer."
12. _____ Refers to a growing body of knowledge that challenges the heterosexual bias in society.

a. transsexuals
b. queer theory
c. asexuality
d. primary sex characteristics
e. heterosexism
f. sexual orientation
g. prostitution
h. bisexuality
i. sex
j. pornography
k. homosexuality
l. intersexed person

Fill-in-the-blank

1. _____ refers to the biological distinction between females and males.
2. One of the twenty-three chromosome pairs found in humans determines one's sex. If the father contributes an (X) chromosome, the offspring will be a _____.
3. _____ *sex characteristics* refer to bodily differences, apart from the genitals, that distinguish biologically mature females and males.
4. Human beings with some combination of female and male genitalia are referred to as _____ people.
5. One cultural universal–an element found in every society the world over–is the _____ _____, a norm forbidding sexual relations or marriage between certain relatives.
6. The most recent studies, show that _____ percent of *teenage boys* and _____ percent of *teenage girls* were sexually active.
7. Some research suggests that *sexual orientation* is rooted in biology. Simon LeVay links sexual orientation to the structure of the _____ _____.
8. Given current scientific research evidence, the best guess at present is that *sexual orientation* is derived from both _____ and _____.
9. The difference between the women who had children in their teens during the 1950s and those who do so today is that during the 1950s, the mothers were much more likely to be _____.
10. _____ describes the fear of close personal interaction with people thought to be gay, lesbian, or bisexual.
11. Traditionally, people have criticized *pornography* on _____ grounds. Today, however, pornography is seen as a _____ issue because it depicts women as the sexual playthings of men.
12. At the bottom of the *sex-worker hierarchy* are _____ _____.
13. *Communication in a public place for the purpose of engaging in prostitution* is against the law in Canada, but many people consider it a _____ *crime*.

14. The term *date rape* highlights the fact that most forced sexual activity involve people who_____ each other.

Definition and Short-Answer
1. What are the important anatomical differences between *males* and *females*? In what ways are these differences important in terms of the relative statuses and roles of women and men in social institutions such as the family and the economy?
2. What evidence was used by Alfred Kinsey to suggest considerable *cultural variation* exists in terms of sexual practices?
3. What are the functions served by the *incest taboo* for both individuals and society as a whole?
4. What do the authors mean by saying that sexual attitudes in Canada are both *restrictive* and *permissive*?
5. When was the *sexual revolution*? What social and cultural factors influenced this revolution? What was the *sexual counterrevolution*? What social and cultural factors helped bring it about?
6. How would you summarize our society's attitudes concerning *premarital sex*?
7. What does Alfred Kinsey mean by the *sexual orientation continuum*? What are the data he uses to argue for its existence?
8. What is the evidence that sexual orientation is a *product of society*? What is the evidence that it is a *product of biology*?
9. Why do you think *teen pregnancy* rates are lower in Canada than in the United States but higher than in many other high-income countries?
10. To what extent would you agree that *pornography* today is less a moral issue than it is an issue concerning power? Why?
11. Is *prostitution* really a victimless crime? Why?
12. What are the *functions* of prostitution for society?
13. Why is it important for society to *regulate* sexuality?
14. What evidence do symbolic-interactionists use to suggest sexuality is *socially constructed*?
15. Social-conflict theorists argue that sexuality is at the root of *inequality* between women and men. How is this so?

PART VI: ANSWERS TO STUDY QUESTIONS

True-False

1. T (p. 153)	6. T (p. 156)	11. F (p. 159)	16. T (p. 165)
2. T (p. 154)	7. T (p. 156)	12. T (p. 159)	17. F (p. 165)
3. F (p. 155)	8. F (pp.156-157)	13. F (p. 160)	18. T (p. 168)
4. F (p. 155)	9. F (p. 158)	14. F (p. 162)	19. T (p. 168)
5. T (p. 155)	10. T (p. 158)	15. T (p. 164)	20. T (p. 173)

Society: The Basics, Second Canadian Edition

Multiple-Choice

1. b (p. 154)
2. c (p. 154)
3. d (p. 155)
4. e (p. 156)
5. c (p. 157)
6. d (p. 157)
7. c (p. 158)
8. e (p. 160)
9. a (p. 160)
10. b (p. 161)
11. e (p. 163)
12. e (p. 163)
13. d (p. 165)
14. c (p. 165)
15. b (p. 166)
16. b (p. 167)
17. d (pp. 168-170)
18. b (p. 171)
19. d (pp. 170-171)
20. c (pp. 168-170)

Matching

1. i (p. 154)
2. d (p. 155)
3. l (p. 155)
4. a (p. 155)
5. f (p. 160)
6. k (p. 160)
7. c (p. 161)
8. h (p. 161)
9. j (p. 164)
10. g (p. 164)
11. e (p. 171)
12. b (p. 171)

Fill-in-the-blank

1. Sex (p. 154)
2. female (p. 154)
3. Secondary (p. 155)
4. Intersexed (p. 163)
5. incest taboo (p. 156)
6. 62, 49 (p. 159)
7. human brain (p. 161)
8. society, biology (p. 161)
9. married (p. 163)
10. Homophobia (p. 163)
11. moral, power (p. 164)
12. street walkers (p. 165)
13. victimless (pp. 165-166)
14. know (p. 168)

PART VII: IN FOCUS – MAJOR ISSUES

1. Differentiate between sex as a *biological issue* and as a *cultural issue*.

2. What evidence exists to support the theory that there is considerable variation in *sexual practices* around the world?

3. What do the authors mean by saying that our cultural orientation toward sexuality has always been *inconsistent*?

4. How strong do you believe the *sexual double standard* is in our society today?

5. What does the research cited in the text suggest about behavioural patterns for each of the following?
   A. Premarital Sex

   B. Sex among Adults

   C. Extramarital Sex

6. What is the evidence concerning each of the following in terms of giving us our sexual orientation?
   A. Biology

   B. Society

Society: The Basics, Second Canadian Edition

7. How have attitudes toward *homosexuality* changed in our society over the last fifty years? What factors have influenced our society's attitudes toward homosexuality?

8. Identify two major points made in the text concerning each of the following four controversial issues:
   A. Teen Pregnancy

   B. Pornography

   C. Prostitution

   D. Sexual Violence

9. According to *structural-functionalists*, why is it important for society to regulate sexuality?

10. What are some *latent functions* of prostitution?

11. Can you think of two latent functions of *pornography*? What are they?

12. Provide an illustration of how global comparisons can be used to illustrate the symbolic-interactionists' view that sexuality is *socially constructed*.

13. According to social-conflict theorists, how is sexuality involved in the creation and maintenance of *social inequality*?

PART VIII: ANALYSIS AND COMMENT

Critical Thinking
"Sex Education: Solution or Problem?"

Key Points: Questions:

Window on the World – Global Map 7-1
"Prostitution in Global Perspective"

Key Points: Questions:

Society: The Basics, Second Canadian Edition

Global Sociology
"Sexual Slavery: A Report from Thailand"
Key Points: Questions:

Critical Thinking
"Date Rape: Exposing Dangerous Myths"
Key Points: Questions:

Controversy and Debate
"The Abortion Controversy"
Key Points: Questions:

Social Stratification

PART I: CHAPTER OUTLINE

1. What is Social Stratification?
2. Caste and Class Systems
    A. The Caste System
    B. The Class System
    C. Classless Societies?
    D. Ideology: The Power Behind Stratification
3. The Functions of Social Stratification
    A. The Davis-Moore Thesis
4. Stratification and Conflict
    A. Karl Marx: Class Conflict
    B. Why No Marxist Revolution?
    C. Max Weber: Class, Status, and Power
5. Stratification and Technology: A Global Perspective
6. Inequality in Canada
    A. Income, Wealth, and Power
    B. Occupational Prestige
    C. Schooling
    D. Ancestry, Race, and Gender
7. Social Classes in Canada
    A. The Upper Class
    B. The Middle Class
    C. The Working Class
    D. The Lower Class
8. The Difference Class Makes
    A. Health
    B. Values and Attitudes
    C. Family and Gender
9. Social Mobility
    A. Myth Versus Reality
    B. Mobility By Income Level
    C. Mobility by Gender
    D. The Global Economy and the Canadian Class Structure

10. Poverty in Canada
    A. The Extent of Poverty
    B. Who are the Poor?
    C. Explaining Poverty
    D. Homelessness
    E. Class and Welfare, Politics and Values
11. Summary
12. Key Concepts
13. Critical-Thinking Questions
14. Applications and Exercises
15. Sites to See

PART II: LEARNING OBJECTIVES
1. To understand the four basic principles of social stratification.
2. To be able to differentiate between the caste and class system of stratification.
3. To begin to understand the relationship between ideology and stratification.
4. To be able to differentiate between the structural-functional and social-conflict perspectives of stratification.
5. To be able to describe the views of Max Weber concerning the dimensions of social class.
6. To be able to describe the approach to understanding social stratification as presented by the Lenskis.
7. To develop a sense of the extent of social inequality in Canada.
8. To consider the meaning of the concept of socioeconomic status and to be aware of its dimensions.
9. To be able to review the role of economic resources, power and occupational prestige, and schooling in the Canadian class system.
10. To be able to identify and trace the significance of various ascribed statuses for the construction and maintenance of social stratification in Canada.
11. To begin to see the significance of the global economy and its impact on our economic system.
12. To be able to generally describe the various social classes in our social stratification system.
13. To become aware of how health, values, family life, and gender are related to the social-class system in our society.
14. To begin to develop a sociological understanding about the nature of social mobility in Canada.
15. To develop a general understanding of the demographics of poverty in Canada.
16. To become aware and critical of different explanations of poverty.
17. To develop an awareness of the problem of homelessness in Canada.
18. To consider some of the dilemmas involved in public assistance and welfare reform.

PART III: KEY CONCEPTS

absolute poverty

alienation

blue-collar occupations

capitalists

caste system

class system

culture of poverty

Davis-Moore thesis

feminization of poverty

ideology

intergenerational social mobility

intragenerational social mobility

market income

meritocracy

proletariat

relative poverty

social mobility

social stratification

socioeconomic status

status consistency

structural social mobility

wealth

white-collar occupations

Society: The Basics, Second Canadian Edition

PART IV: IMPORTANT RESEARCHERS

Karl Marx   Herbert Spencer

Gerhard and Jean Lenski   Ralph Dahrendorf

Plato   William Julius Wilson

Melvin Tumin   Oscar Lewis

Max Weber

PART V: STUDY QUESTIONS

True-False

1. T F Social stratification is *universal*–found in all societies.
2. T F *Ascription* is fundamental to social-stratification systems based on *castes*.
3. T F *Caste systems* tend to be characterized by *endogamous marriages*.
4. T F The *working class* is the largest segment of the population in *Great Britain*.
5. T F *Ideology* refers to cultural beliefs that serve to justify social stratification.

6. T F   The ancient Greek philosopher *Plato* defined *justice* as agreement about who should have what.
7. T F   The *Davis-Moore thesis* is a component of the social-conflict perspective of social stratification.
8. T F   *Structural-functionalists* argue that social stratification encourages a matching of talents and abilities to appropriate positions in society.
9. T F   *Karl Marx's* social conflict theory of social stratification identified two basic relationships to the means of production—those who own productive property, and those who labour for others.
10. T F Unlike Karl Marx, *Max Weber* believed that socialism would increase inequality by expanding government and concentrating power in the hands of political elite.
11. T F *Gerhard* and *Jean Lenski* argued that hunting and gathering societies have greater social inequality than agrarian or horticultural societies.
12. T F The *Kuznets curve* projects greater social inequality as industrial societies advance technologically.
13. T F *Wealth* in Canada is distributed more equally than income.
14. T F *Wealth* is defined as the total value of money and other assets, minus outstanding debts.
15. T F Half of Canadian families earned more than $77 910 in 1995.
16. T F Only about 50 percent of adults in Canada have a high school diploma.
17. T F About 20 percent of Canadian adults have a college or university degree.
18. T F The *working class* is the largest social class in Canada.
19. T F Affluent people are less openly tolerant of controversial behaviour than are working class people.
20. T F The long-term trend in social mobility has been upward.
21. T F All income groups had higher incomes in 1998 when compared to 1980.
22. T F A family of four living in a large urban area would have to earn more than $46 500 in order to rise above the poverty line (LICO).
23. T F Almost 8 percent of Canadians lived below the poverty line in 1998.
24. T F The elderly are at the greatest risk for poverty.
25. T F Almost one in four aboriginal youths aged 6 to 14 is poor.
26. T F The *culture of poverty* is a concept relating poverty to a lower-class subculture that inhibits personal achievement and fosters resignation.
27. T F William Julius Wilson believes that the solution to the problems of inner cities is the *creation of jobs*.
28. T F Most poor families in Canada do not have a wage earner.
29. T F People in Canada are just as likely to blame individuals as they are to blame society for the existence of poverty in our country.
30. T F It is estimated that, annually, there are about 2000 homeless youth in Toronto.

Multiple Choice

1. A system by which a society ranks categories of people in a hierarchy is called
   a) social inequality.
   b) meritocracy.
   c) social stratification.
   d) social mobility.

2. Which of the following principles is *not* a basic factor in explaining the existence of social stratification?
   a) Although universal, social stratification also varies in form.
   b) Social stratification persists over generations.
   c) Social stratification rests on widely held beliefs.
   d) Social stratification is a characteristic of society, not simply a function of individual differences.
   e) All are factors in explaining social stratification.

3. A change in one's position in a social hierarchy refers to
   a) ideology.
   b) social mobility.
   c) meritocracy.
   d) social inequality.
   e) endogamy.

4. What is a *caste system*?
   a) social stratification based on ascription
   b) social stratification based on meritocracy
   c) social stratification based on achievement
   d) any system in which there is social inequality

5. Which of the following is *not* one of the four *castes* in India's traditional caste system?
   a) Vaishya
   b) Jaishra
   c) Shudra
   d) Brahmin
   e) Kshatriya

6. In a *caste system*, birth shapes people's lives in all but which of the following ways?
   a) Traditional caste groups have specific occupations.
   b) Castes require the norm of exogamous marriages.
   c) Caste norms guide people to stay in the company of "their own kind."
   d) Caste systems rest on powerful cultural beliefs.

7. Which characteristics that follow are most accurate of *class systems*?
   a) They are more clearly defined than castes.
   b) They have variable status consistency.
   c) They have occupations based on ascription.
   d) All of the above.

8. *Apartheid* became law in South Africa in
   a) 1916.
   b) 1971.
   c) 1948.
   d) 1876.

9. What is the term for the degree of consistency in a person's social standing across various dimensions of social inequality?
   a) status consonance
   b) status congruity
   c) status balance
   d) status consistency
   e) socioeconomic status

10. In the Middle Ages, social stratification in England was a system of three
    a) open classes.
    b) absolute castes.
    c) meritocracies.
    d) closed classes.
    e) caste-like estates.

11. The social stratification system in the United Kingdom today still has vestiges of its feudal system of the past. Which of the following was characteristic of their feudal system?
    a) It was a caste-like estate system.
    b) It was based on the law of primogeniture.
    c) It consisted of the nobility, the clergy, and the commoners.
    d) all of the above

12. The *United Kingdom* today is identified as a(n)
    a) neomonarchy.
    b) caste system.
    c) estate system.
    d) open estate system.
    e) class society.

13. Which of the following comprises one-half of all persons in the United Kingdom's class system?
    a) working class
    b) upper class
    c) lower class
    d) middle class

14. The former Soviet Union had four levels in their social stratification system. The highest level was known as
    a) intelligentsia.
    b) perestroika.
    c) apparatchiks.
    d) primogeniture.
    e) nogoodniks.

15. What do sociologists call a shift in the social position of large numbers of people due more to changes in society itself than to individual efforts?
    a) perestroika
    b) bureaucratization
    c) linear social stratification
    d) structural social mobility

16. What is *ideology*?
    a) a system in which entire categories of people are ranked in a hierarchy
    b) ideas that are generated through scientific investigation
    c) views and opinions that are based on the principle of cultural relativism
    d) ideas that limit the amount of inequality of a society
    e) cultural beliefs that serve to justify social stratification

17. The *Davis-Moore thesis* asserts that
    a) social stratification has beneficial consequences for the operation of society.
    b) industrialization produces greater, and more harmful social stratification than previous forms of subsistence.
    c) social stratification based on meritocracy has dysfunctional consequences for society and its individual members.
    d) ideology undermines social stratification.
    e) industrial capitalism is moving toward a classless social order.

18. Which perspective of social stratification views social inequality as the domination of some categories of people by others?
    a) symbolic-interactionism
    b) sociocultural evolution
    c) social-conflict
    d) structural-functionalism

19. In Karl Marx's analysis of social stratification, another name for the working class is the
    a) primogeniture.
    b) perestroika.
    c) apparatchiks.
    d) proletariat.
    e) bourgeoisie.

20. Which of the following is/are reasons given as to why there has been *no Marxist revolution*?
    a) the fragmentation of the capitalist class
    b) a higher standard of living
    c) more extensive worker organization
    d) more extensive legal protections
    e) all of the above

21. Which of the following is *not* one of the dimensions of social stratification according to Max Weber?
    a) class
    b) education
    c) power
    d) status

22. According to the model of *sociocultural evolution* developed by *Gerhard* and *Jean Lenski*, social stratification is at its peak in
    a) hunting and gathering societies.
    b) post-industrial societies.
    c) large-scale agrarian societies.
    d) industrial societies.

23. The *Kuznets curve* suggests
    a) industrialization and social stratification are unrelated.
    b) industrial societies are represented by greater social inequality than agrarian societies.
    c) the emergence of post-industrial society may signal greater social inequality.
    d) greater technological sophistication is generally accompanied by greater social equality.

24. Which of the following is/are accurate statements?
    a) Generally speaking, countries that have had centralized, socialist economies display the least income inequality.
    b) The standard of living in countries that have had centralized, socialist economies tend to have a relatively low standard of living.
    c) Industrial societies with capitalist economies have higher overall living standards compared to other countries.
    d) Severe income disparity characterizes industrial societies with capitalist economies.
    e) all of the above

25. Statistics show that *income* is unequally distributed in Canada. Which of the following statements is most accurate?
    a) The average household income in Canada in 1998 was $55 224.
    b) The top 20 percent of households (by income) receive sixty-five percent of the income earned in Canada.
    c) The poorest twenty percent of households receive only ten percent of the income earned in Canada.
    d) Wealth is distributed more equally in Canada than is income.

26. The wealthiest 20 percent of Canadian families own roughly ____ percent of the countries wealth.
    a) 80
    b) 60
    c) 40
    d) 20

27. Visible minorities tend to have _____ education and _____ income than other Canadians.
    a) higher/lower
    b) lower/higher
    c) lower/lower
    d) higher/higher

28. The upper 5 percent of Canadian families earn at least
    a) $100 000
    b) $120 000
    c) $140 000
    d) $160 000
    e) $180 000

29. The *middle class* includes approximately what percentage of the Canadian population?
    a) 20-25
    b) 40-45
    c) 30-35
    d) 55-60

30. Well-off people tend to be more _____ on economic issues but/and more _____ on social issues than those less well-off.
    a) conservative/conservative
    b) liberal/liberal
    c) conservative/liberal
    d) liberal/conservative

31. A change in social position of children relative to that of their parents is called
    a) horizontal social mobility.
    b) structural social mobility.
    c) intergenerational social mobility.
    d) intragenerational social mobility.

32. What does research reveal about *social mobility* in Canada?
    a) Social mobility, at least among men, has been relatively low.
    b) The long-term trend in social mobility has been downward.
    c) Within a single generation, social mobility is usually dramatic, not incremental.
    d) The short-term trend has been stagnation, with some income polarization.

33. The earning difference between men and women has narrowed over the last 40 years because, while the income of women increased, the income of men
    a) consistently increased but at a lower rate.
    b) remained constant.
    c) declined for long periods.
    d) remained unchanged.

34. High-paying jobs in *manufacturing* accounted for 31 percent of jobs in 1951; today, such jobs support _____ percent of our workforce.
    a) 15
    b) 20
    c) 25
    d) 30
    e) 35

35. Approximately what percentage of the Canadian population is officially classified as being poor?
    a) 5
    b) 12
    c) 19
    d) 26

36. Poverty statistics in Canada reveal that
    a) the elderly are more likely than any other age group to be poor.
    b) almost 70 percent of all Aboriginals are poor.
    c) urban and suburban poverty rates are lower than rural poverty rates.
    d) about 55 percent of the poor are female.

37. The *culture of poverty* view concerning the causes of poverty
    a) holds that the poor are primarily responsible for their own poverty.
    b) blames poverty on economic stagnation relating to the globalization of the Canadian economy.
    c) sees lack of ambition on the part of the poor as a consequence, not a cause of poverty.
    d) views the conservative economic policies of the last two decades in Canada as the primary reason for relatively high poverty rates.

38. Almost all homeless have one thing in common:
    a) poverty
    b) age
    c) gender
    d) ethnicity

39. Advocates for the homeless argue that societal factors cause homelessness and point to which of the following as evidence?
    a) lack of low-income housing
    b) unemployment
    c) increasing number of low-income jobs
    d) all of the above

40. Which is the fastest-growing subcategory among the homeless?
    a) children
    b) elderly women
    c) elderly men
    d) families

Society: The Basics, Second Canadian Edition

Matching

1. _____ The total value of money and other assets, minus outstanding debts.
2. _____ Encompasses forty to fifty-five percent of the Canadian population and exerts tremendous influence on Canadian culture.
3. _____ Accounts for about one-third of the Canadian population.
4. _____ A change in social position occurring within a person's lifetime.
5. _____ Upward or downward social mobility of children in relation to their parents.
6. _____ Especially for women, usually signal downward social mobility.
7. _____ The deprivation of some people in relation to those who have more.
8. _____ Describes the trend by which women represent an increasing proportion of the poor.
9. _____ Developed the concept of the *culture of poverty*, or a lower-class subculture that inhibits personal achievement and fosters resignation to one's plight.
10. _____ Argued that *society* is primarily responsible for poverty and that any lack of ambition on the part of the poor is a *consequence* of insufficient opportunity.
11. _____ According to Karl Marx, the people who own and operate factories and other productive businesses in pursuit of profit.
12. _____ The assertion that social stratification is universal because it has beneficial consequences for the operation of society.
13. _____ The degree of consistency in a person's social standing across various dimensions of social inequality.
14. _____ According to Karl Marx, the people who sell their productive labour for wages.
15. _____ Social stratification based on *ascription*.
16. _____ Cultural beliefs that justify social stratification.
17. _____ Reveals that greater *technological* sophistication is generally accompanied by more pronounced *social-stratification*, to a point.
18. _____ Developed a multidimensional model of social class which included the variables of *class*, *status*, and *power*.
19. _____ An economic program, meaning *restructuring*, developed by Mikhail Gorbachev.
20. _____ The experience of isolation and misery resulting from powerlessness.

a. William Julius Wilson
b. intergenerational social mobility
c. feminization of poverty
d. wealth
e. intragenerational social mobility
f. the working-class
g. Oscar Lewis
h. the middle-class
i divorce
j. relative poverty
k. ideology
l. capitalists
m. the Davis-Moore thesis
n status consistency
o. perestroika
p. caste
q. Kuznets curve
r. Max Weber
s. proletariat
t. alienation

Fill-in-the-blank

1. *Social* _____ refers to a system by which a society ranks categories of people in a hierarchy.

2. Social stratification is a matter of four *basic principles*: it is a trait of _____, not simply a reflection of individual differences; it _____ over generations; it is _____ but variable; and, it involves not just inequality but _____.

3. Caste systems mandate that people marry others of the same ranking. Sociologists call this pattern _____ *marriage*.

4. Whereas a _____ is a system of social stratification based *ascription*, a _____ is a system in which social position is based entirely on *personal merit*.

5. In the feudal past of the United Kingdom, the *law of* _____ mandated that only the eldest son inherited property of parents.

6. _____ *social mobility* refers to a shift in the social position of large numbers of people due more to changes in society itself than to individual efforts.

7. _____ refers to cultural beliefs that justify social stratification.

8. According to Karl Marx, capitalism produces _____, or the experience of isolation and misery resulting from powerlessness.

9. Four reasons are given as to why there has been *no Marxist revolution*, including: the _____ of the capitalist class, a _____ standard of living, more extensive worker _____, and more extensive legal _____.

10. Advocates of *social-conflict analysis* believe that Karl Marx's analysis of capitalism is still largely valid. They offer the following reasons: wealth remains largely _____, _____ work offers little to workers, progress requires _____, and the _____ still favours the rich.

Society: The Basics, Second Canadian Edition

11. The three components of *Max Weber's* model of social class are _____, _____, and _____.

12. _____ *status* refers to a composite ranking based on various dimensions of social inequality.

13. Gerhard and Jean Lenski argue that the level of _____ representative of a society is a very significant factor in determining the nature of social stratification in that society.

14. The richest twenty percent of families in Canada control _____ percent of all wealth.

15. _____ is the total value of money and other assets, minus outstanding debts.

16. When financial assets are balanced against debts, the lowest-ranking _____ percent of Canadian families have virtually no *wealth* at all.

17. The *average family income* for Canadian families in 1998 was $_____.

18. The *working-class* comprises about _____ percent of the Canadian population.

19. In 1998, _____ percent of our population lived below the poverty line.

20. While the relationship between social class and politics is complex, generally, members of high social standing tend to have _____ *views on economic issues* and _____ *views on social issues*.

21. _____ *social mobility* refers to a change in social position occurring within a person's lifetime.

22. _____ *poverty* refers to deprivation of some people in relation to those who have more.

23. For a family of four living in a large urban centre, in 1998, the poverty threshold was _____.

24. _____ percent of the poor in Canada are over the age of sixty-five.

130

25. The trend by which females represent an increasing proportion of the poor is called the _____ *of poverty*.
26. In Canada in 1997, _____ percent of *children* were poor.
27. William Julius Wilson sees any apparent lack of ambition on the part of the poor as a _____ of insufficient opportunity rather than a _____ of poverty.
28. Virtually all *homeless people* have one status in common: _____.
29. The authors argue that the weight of the sociological evidence points towards _____ as the primary source of poverty because the poor are _____ of people.
30. About the same number of Canadians attribute poverty to personal _____ as do those who attribute poverty to societal _____.

Definition and Short-Answer
1. What are the four *fundamental principles* of social stratification?
2. Briefly describe the social-stratification system of *Great Britain*.
3. What are the four reasons given in the text for why the *Marxist Revolution* has not occurred?
4. What are the basic qualities of a *caste system*?
5. What is meant by the concept *structural social mobility*? Provide two illustrations.
6. What are the components of *Max Weber's* multidimensional model of social stratification? Define each.
7. What are some of the characteristics of the *Davis-Moore thesis*? What is your opinion of this thesis and its relevance for helping us understand our social stratification? What evidence exists in support of this thesis? What evidence contradicts it?
8. What are some of the reasons why people in Canada might tend to underestimate the extent of social inequality in our society?
9. How are *wealth* and *income* distributed throughout the population in Canada?
10. What are the basic components of *socioeconomic status*? How are they measured? How do these components differ from Max Weber's components of social class?
11. To what extent do *ascribed statuses* affect a person's place in our social-stratification system? Provide examples using the variables of race, ethnicity, and gender.
12. Using the factors of health, values, and politics, discuss the difference social class makes in the lives of people within our society.
13. Identify six significant *demographic characteristics* of the poor in our society today.

14. What is meant by the term *culture of poverty*? What policies and programs do you think could be instituted to counteract this phenomenon?
15. What is meant by the term *feminization of poverty*? What can be done to reverse this trend in our society?
16. Review the basic points being made by *Gerhard* and *Jean Lenski* concerning global inequality in historical perspective.
17. What are the four general conclusions being made about *social mobility* in Canada today?

PART VI: ANSWERS TO STUDY QUESTIONS

True-False

1. T (p. 178)	9. T (p. 185)	17. F (p. 191)	24. F (p. 199)
2. T (p. 178)	10. T (p. 187)	18. F (p. 193)	25. F (p. 199)
3. T (p. 179)	11. F (p. 188)	19. F (p. 194)	26. T (p. 199)
4. T (p. 181)	12. F (p. 188)	20. T (p. 196)	27. T (p. 199)
5. T (p. 183)	13. F (p. 190)	21. F (p. 196)	28. F (p. 201)
6. T (p. 183)	14. T (p. 190)	22. F (p. 198)	29. T (p. 201)
7. F (p. 183)	15. F (p. 191)	23. F (p. 198)	30. F (p. 201)
8. T (p. 184)	16. F (p. 191)		

Multiple Choice

1. c (p. 178)	11. d (p. 181)	21. b (p. 187)	31. c (p. 195)
2. e (p. 178)	12. e (p. 181)	22. c (p. 188)	32. d (p. 196)
3. b (p. 178)	13. a (p. 181)	23. c (p. 188)	33. c (p. 197)
4. a (p. 178)	14. c (p. 182)	24. e (p. 188)	34. b (p. 198)
5. b (p. 178)	15. e (p. 182)	25. a (p. 190)	35. b (p. 198)
6. b (p. 179)	16. d (p. 183)	26. a (p. 190)	36. d (p. 199)
7. b (p. 179)	17. a (p. 183)	27. a (p. 191)	37. a (p. 199)
8. c (p. 180)	18. c (p. 184)	28. b (p. 192)	38. a (p. 201)
9. d (p. 180)	19. d (p. 185)	29. b (p. 193)	39. d (p. 202)
10. e (p. 181)	20. e (p. 186)	30. c (p. 195)	40. a (p. 202)

Matching

1. d (p. 190)	6. i (p. 195)	11. l (p. 185)	16. k (p. 183)
2. h (p. 193)	7. j (p. 198)	12. m (p. 183)	17. q (p. 188)
3. f (p. 193)	8. c (p. 199)	13. n (p. 180)	18. r (p. 187)
4. e (p. 195)	9. g (p. 199)	14. s (p. 185)	19. o (p. 182)
5. b (p. 195)	10. a (p. 199)	15. p (p. 178)	20. t (p. 185)

Fill-in-the-blank

1. stratification (p. 178)
2. society, persists, universal, beliefs (p. 178)
3. endogamous (p. 179)
4. caste, meritocracy (pp. 178-179)
5. primogeniture (p. 181)
6. Structural (p. 182)
7. Ideology (p. 183)

8. alienation (p. 185)
9. fragmentation, higher, organization, protection (p. 186)
10. concentrated, white-collar, struggle, law (pp. 186-187)
11. class, status, power (p. 187)
12. Socioeconomic (p. 187)
13. technology (p. 188)
14. 80 (p.190)
15. wealth (p. 190)
16. 30 (p. 190)
17. $55 224 (p. 190)
18. 33 (p. 193)
19. 12.2 (p. 198)
20. conservative, liberal (p. 195)
21. intragenerational (p. 195)
22. relative (p. 198)
23. $27 890 (p.198)
24. 13 (p. 199)
25. feminization (p. 199)
26. 19.8 (p. 199)
27. consequence, cause (p. 199)
28. poverty (p. 201)
29. society, categories (p. 201)
30. laziness, injustice (p. 201)

PART VII: IN FOCUS—IMPORTANT ISSUES

1. What is *social stratification*?

2. What are the four basic *principles of social stratification*?
    A.

    B.

    C.

    D.

3. Identify three major characteristics of a *caste system*.

4. Identify three major characteristics of a *class system*.

5. What is the *Davis-Moore thesis*? What do critics argue about this structural-functionalist view of social stratification? What is the evidence that this thesis is valid?

6. What was Karl Marx's argument about *class and conflict*?

7. What is the evidence that Marx's view is still relevant today?

8. What are four reasons why a *Marxist Revolution* has not occurred in capitalist societies?

9. What are the four general conclusions about *social mobility* in Canada being made in the text?

Study Guide

10. Define each of the three *dimensions of social stratification* as identified by Max Weber.
    A. Class

    B. Status

    C. Power

11. Provide evidence of *social inequality* in Canada for the following variables—making reference to *Figures 8-3 and 8-4, and Table 8-2*.
    A. Income

    B. Wealth

    C. Education

12. Identify three or four general characteristics for each of the following *social classes*.
    A. The Upper Class

    B. The Middle Class

C. The Working Class

D. The Lower Class

13. Briefly describe how social class *makes a difference* in the following domains of life.
    A. Health

    B. Values and Attitudes

    C. Family Patterns

14. What are pieces of evidence given in the text for a slowing in upward social mobility in Canada?

15. Who are the *poor*? (general demographic patterns in Canada today)
    A. Age

    B. Race and Ethnicity

    C. Gender and Family Patterns

D. Rural and Urban Poverty

16. How is poverty to be *explained*?

17. What is the evidence that the poor are primarily responsible for their own poverty?

18. What is the evidence that society is primarily responsible for poverty?

PART VIII: ANALYSIS AND COMMENT

Global Sociology
"Race as Caste: A Report From South Africa"
Key Points: Questions:

Applying Sociology
"Is Getting Rich 'The Survival of the Fittest'?"
Key Points: Questions:

Society: The Basics, Second Canadian Edition

Window on the World – Global Map 8-1
"Income Disparity in Global Perspective"
Key Points: Questions:

Seeing Ourselves—National Map 8-1
"Average Income Across Canada, 1995"
Key Points: Questions:

Seeing Ourselves—National Map 8-2
"Percentage of Families Below the Poverty Line, Canada, 1995"
Key Points: Questions:

Controversy and Debate
"The Bell Curve Debate: Are Rich People Really Smarter?"
Key Points: Questions:

Global Stratification

PART I: CHAPTER OUTLINE

1. Global Stratification: An Overview
   A. A Word About Terminology
   B. High-Income Countries
   C. Middle-Income Countries
   D. Low-Income Countries
2. Global Wealth and Poverty
   A. The Severity of Poverty
   B. The Extent of Poverty
   C. Poverty and Children
   D. Poverty and Women
   E. Slavery
   F. Correlates of Global Poverty
3. Global Stratification: Theoretical Analysis
   A. Modernization Theory
   B. Dependency Theory
4. Global Inequality: Looking Ahead
5. Summary
6. Key Concepts
7. Critical-Thinking Questions
8. Applications and Exercises
9. Sites to See

PART II: LEARNING OBJECTIVES

1. To be able to define and describe the demographics of the three "economic development" categories used to classify nations of the world.
2. To begin to understand both the severity and extensiveness of poverty in the low-income nations of the world.
3. To recognize the extent to which women are overrepresented among the poor of the world and the factors leading to this condition.
4. To be able to identify and discuss the correlates of global poverty.
5. To be able to identify and discuss the two major theories used to explain global inequality.
6. To be able to identify and describe the stages of modernization.

Society: The Basics, Second Canadian Edition

7. To be able to recognize the problems facing women as a result of modernization in the low-income nations of the world.
8. To be able to identify the keys to combating global inequality over the next century.

PART III: KEY CONCEPTS

colonialism

dependency theory

modernization theory

multinational corporation

neocolonialism

PART IV: IMPORTANT RESEARCHERS

Immanuel Wallerstein   W. W. Rostow

PART V: STUDY QUESTIONS

True-False

1. T F Because global income is so concentrated, even people in Canada with incomes below the poverty line (LICO) live better than the majority of the earth's people.
2. T F The wealth of the world's three *richest people* equals the annual economic output of the world's forty-eight poorest countries.
3. T F The *Second World* now includes most of Europe.
4. T F The *high-income countries* include the 150 richest countries in the world.
5. T F Approximately 40 percent of the world's population live in *low-income countries*.
6. T F Approximately one-third of the population of *low-income countries* lives in urban areas.
7. T F *Low-income countries* are constantly threatened by hunger, unsafe housing, and high rates of disease.
8. T F *Australia* has the highest *quality of life score* in the world.
9. T F A key reason why the *quality of life* differs so much around the world is that economic productivity is lowest in precisely the regions of the globe where population growth is highest.

10. T F *High-income countries* are by far the most advantaged economically, with fifty-six percent of the world's income supporting just fifteen percent of the world's population.

11. T F *Absolute poverty* refers to a lack of resources that is life threatening.

12. T F About 15 percent of the global population suffer from chronic hunger.

13. T F There is a greater disparity of wealth along lines of *gender* in low-income countries than in high-income, industrial societies.

14. T F Only about twenty percent of the people living in *low-income societies* farm the land.

15. T F *Modernization theory* suggests the greatest barrier to economic development is *traditionalism*.

16. T F *Modernization theory* draws criticism for suggesting that the causes of global poverty lie almost entirely in poor societies themselves.

17. T F *Immanuel Wallerstein's* capitalist world economy model is used to illustrate and support *dependency theory*.

18. T F *Dependency theory* claims that the increasing prosperity of high-income countries has largely come at the expense of low-income countries.

19. T F According to *dependency theory*, global inequality must be seen in terms of the distribution of wealth, as opposed to highlighting the productivity of wealth.

20. T F As the low-income countries increase their standard of living, less stress is expected to be placed on the *physical environment*.

21. T F The keys to combating global inequality during the next century lie in seeing it as partly a *problem of technology* and also a *political problem*.

22. T F Ten million of the world's children die each year as a result of *hunger*.

Multiple Choice

1. The wealth of the richest three individuals roughly equals the annual economic output of the world's _____ poorest countries.
   a) 18
   b) 28
   c) 38
   d) 48
   e) 58

2. The *high-income countries*, representing fifteen percent of the world's population, control about _____ percent of the world's income.
   a) 26
   b) 36
   c) 46
   d) 56

3. Which of the following statements concerning *high-income countries* is/are accurate?
   a) Taken together, countries with the most developed economies cover roughly twenty-five percent of the earth's land area.
   b) About three-fourths of the people in high-income countries live in or near cities.
   c) Significant cultural differences exist among high-income countries.
   d) All of the above are accurate statements.

4. Which of the following is an *inaccurate* statement concerning *middle-income countries*?
   a) In middle-income countries, per capita income ranges between $2500 and $14 500.
   b) About half the people in middle-income countries still live in rural areas and work in agriculture.
   c) One cluster of middle-income countries includes the former Soviet Union and the nations of Eastern Europe.
   d) Taken together, middle-income countries span roughly 75 percent of the earth's land area.

5. *Middle-income countries* cover _____ percent of the earth's land area and almost half of humanity.
   a) 10
   b) 20
   c) 30
   d) 40
   e) 50

6. What percentage of the world's population lives in the *low-income countries* of the world?
   a) 20
   b) 40
   c) 60
   d) 80
   e) 95

7. On average, population density is highest in
   a) low-income countries
   b) middle-income countries
   c) high-income countries
   d) rural areas

8. The 1999 per-capita GNP in Canada was
   a) US$13 725
   b) US$18 725
   c) US$23 725
   d) US$28 725
   e) US$33 725

9. Which country has the highest score on the *Quality of Life Index*?
   a) Canada
   b) the United States
   c) Brazil
   d) Germany

10. Half of all deaths in low-income countries occur among
    a) the elderly beyond the age of 65.
    b) young adults 18-35.
    c) adults between the ages of 40 and 59.
    d) children under ten.

11. Which of the following is *inaccurate*?
    a) Families in poor societies do not depend on women's incomes.
    b) In high-income countries, the median age at death is over 75 years of age.
    c) The United Nations estimates that in low-income countries men own ninety percent of the land.
    d) About seventy percent of the world's one billion or more people who live in absolute poverty are female.

12. Which of the following is *not* a type of *slavery* identified in the text?
    a) chattel
    b) child
    c) debt bondage
    d) servile forms of marriage
    e) colonial

13. Which of the following is *not* discussed as a correlate of *global poverty*?
    a) cultural patterns
    b) population growth
    c) technology
    d) social stratification
    e) all are discussed

14. *Neocolonialism* is
    a) primarily an overt political force.
    b) a form of economic exploitation that does not involve formal political control.
    c) the economic power of the low-income countries is being used to control the consumption patterns in the high-income countries.
    d) the exploitation of the high-income countries by the low-income countries.
    e) none of the above

15. A model of economic and social development that explains global inequality in terms of technological and cultural differences among societies is _____ theory.
    a) colonial
    b) dependency
    c) modernization
    d) ecological

16. *Modernization theory* identifies _____ as the greatest barrier to economic development.
    a) technology
    b) social equality
    c) social power
    d) tradition

17. Which of the following is *not* a stage in Rostow's model of modernization?
    a) colonialism
    b) traditional
    c) take-off
    d) drive to technological maturity
    e) high mass consumption

18. According to *W. W. Rostow's* modernization model, which stage is Thailand currently in?
    a) traditional
    b) take-off
    c) drive to technological maturity
    d) high mass consumption
    e) residual-dependency

19. Which of the following is *not* a criticism of modernization theory?
    a) It tends to minimize the connection between rich and poor societies.
    b) It tends to blame the low-income countries for their own poverty.
    c) It ignores historical facts that thwart development in poor countries.
    d) It has fallen short of its own standards of success.
    e) all are criticisms of this theory

20. _____ *theory* is a model of economic and social development that explains global inequality in terms of the historical exploitation of poor societies by rich ones.
    a) Modernization
    b) Colonial
    c) Dependency
    d) Evolutionary
    e) Ecological

21. Which of the following is *not* mentioned in *Immanuel Wallerstein's* capitalist world-economy model as a reason for the perpetuation of the dependency of the low-income countries?
    a) narrow, export-oriented economies
    b) lack of industrial capacity
    c) foreign debt
    d) all are mentioned
    e) none are

22. Which of the following is *not* a criticism of dependency theory?
    a) It assumes that the wealth of the high-income countries is based solely on appropriating resources from low-income societies.
    b) It tends to blame the low-income countries for their own poverty.
    c) It does not lend itself to clear policy making.
    d) It assumes that world capitalism alone has produced global inequality.
    e) all of these are criticisms of this theory

23. In approximately _____ of the world's countries, living standards are lower than they were in 1980.
    a) one-third
    b) one-half
    c) three-fourths
    d) eighty-eight percent

24. Which of the following is an *inaccurate* statement regarding *global stratification*?
    a) According to the United Nations, people in one-third of the world's countries are living far better in 1996 than they were in 1980.
    b) One insight, offered by modernization theory, is that poverty is partly a problem of technology.
    c) One insight, derived from dependency theory, is that global inequality as a problem is also a political issue.
    d) While economic development increases living standards, it also establishes a context for less strain being placed on the physical environment.

Matching
1. _____ A model of economic and social development that explains global inequality in terms of the historical exploitation of poor societies by rich ones.
2. _____ The process by which some nations enrich themselves through political and economic control of other nations.
3. _____ The percentage of people in low-income countries who live in cities.
4. _____ Percentage of the world's income controlled by the 40 percent who live in low-income countries.
5. _____ Two high-income countries.
6. _____ The percentage of the world's population living in high-income countries.
7. _____ Huge businesses that operate in many countries.
8. _____ The percentage of births attended by trained health personnel in Mexico.
9. _____ A model of economic and social development that explains global inequality in terms of technological and cultural differences among societies.
10. _____ Two middle-income countries.

a. Argentina and Malaysia
b. modernization theory
c. multinational corporations
d. colonialism
e. 11
f. 15
g. Canada and Singapore
h. 75
i. dependency theory
j. 30

Society: The Basics, Second Canadian Edition

Fill-in-the-blank

1. Compared to the traditional "three worlds" model, the new classification system used in the text has two main advantages, including a focus on the single most important dimension that underlies social life–_____ _____.

2. The 40 percent of Canadian families with the lowest incomes earn about 20 percent of the national income. The 40 percent of the *global population* that live in low-income countries received _____ percent of the world's income.

3. The *middle-income countries* of the world represent about _____ nations and _____ percent of the world's population.

4. According to our authors, poverty in *low-income countries* is more _____ and more _____ than it is in Canada.

5. Canada had a GNP in 1999 of over _____ U.S. dollars.

6. The four types of slavery identified in the text include: _____, _____, _____ _____, and _____ forms of marriage.

7. The *correlates of global poverty* include _____, population _____, _____ patterns, social _____, _____ inequality, and global _____ relationships.

8. _____ is a new form of economic exploitation that does not involve formal political control.

9. _____ *theorists* suggest global inequality reflects differing levels of technological development and cultural differences among societies.

10. *W. W. Rostow's* stages of modernization include: the _____, _____, drive to _____ maturity, and high mass _____.

11. _____ theory maintains that global poverty historically stems from the exploitation of poor societies by rich societies.

12. Immanuel Wallerstein calls the *rich nations* the _____ of the world economy. He refers to the *low-income* countries as the _____ of the world economy.

13. *Modernization theory* suggests that modern nations _____ _____ through technological innovation.

14. *Dependency theory* views global stratification in terms of how countries _____ _____.

15. In about _____ of the nations of the world, people are enjoying a higher *standard of living* than ever before. The overall pattern in the world however is toward *economic* _____ between the high-income and low-income nations.

16. Two keys to combating global inequality during the next century will be seeing it partly as a problem of _____ and that it is also a _____ problem.

Definition and Short-Answer

1. Define the terms *high-income*, *middle-income*, and *low-income countries*. Identify the key characteristics of each category. Does this resolve the "terminology" problem?
2. How do the economies in each of the three *levels* or *categories* of countries differ from one another? Make specific reference to *Figures 9-1* and *9-2* in your answer.
3. What factors create the condition of *women* being overrepresented in poverty around the world?
4. What are the *correlates* of global poverty? Describe each.
5. What is *neocolonialism*? Provide an illustration.
6. What are the four stages of *modernization* in Rostow's model of societal change and development?
7. What are the *problems* faced by women in poor countries as a result of modernization?
8. According to *modernization* theorists, in what respects are high-income nations part of the solution to global poverty?

Society: The Basics, Second Canadian Edition

9. Differentiate between how *modernization theory* and *dependency theory* view the primary causes of global inequality. Critique each of these theories, identifying the strengths and weaknesses of each in terms of explaining global poverty. How does each differ in terms of recommendations to improve the conditions in low-income countries?

10. Write an essay about *poverty in low-income countries*. What are the statistics of *global poverty*?

PART VI: ANSWERS TO STUDY QUESTIONS

True-False
1. T (p. 207)
2. T (p. 207)
3. F (p. 207)
4. F (p. 208)
5. T (p. 210)
6. T (p. 210)
7. T (p. 210)
8. F (p. 211)
9. T (p. 211)
10. T (p. 212)
11. T (p. 212)
12. T (p. 212)
13. T (pp.212-213)
14. F (p. 214)
15. T (p. 216)
16. T (p. 219)
17. T (p. 220)
18. T (p. 220)
19. T (p. 221)
20. F (p. 224)
21. T (p. 224)
22. T (p. 226)

Multiple Choice
1. d (p. 207)
2. d (p. 212)
3. d (p. 208)
4. d (p. 209)
5. e (p. 209)
6. b (p. 210)
7. c (p. 210)
8. c (p. 211)
9. a (p. 211)
10. d (p. 212)
11. a (pp.212-213)
12. e (p. 214)
13. e (p. 214)
14. b (p. 215)
15. c (p. 216)
16. d (p. 216)
17. a (pp.217-218)
18. b (p. 218)
19. e (pp.219-220)
20. c (p. 220)
21. d (p. 221)
22. b (pp.222-223)
23. a (p. 224)
24. d (p. 224)

Matching
1. i (p. 220)
2. d (p. 215)
3. j (p. 210)
4. e (p. 212)
5. g (p. 208)
6. f (p. 212)
7. c (p. 215)
8. h (p. 214)
9. b (p. 216)
10. a (p. 211)

Fill-in-the-blank
1. economic development (p. 208)
2. 11 (p. 212)
3. 90, 44 (p. 208, 212)
4. severe, extensive (p. 210)
5. 726 billion (p. 211)
6. chattel, child, debt bondage, servile (p. 214)
7. technology, growth, cultural, stratification, gender, power (pp. 214-215)
8. neocolonialism (p. 215)
9. Modernization (p. 216)
10. traditional, take-off, technological, consumption (pp. 217-218)
11. Dependency (p. 220)
12. core, periphery (pp. 220-221)
13. produce wealth (p. 221)
14. distribute wealth (p. 221)
15. one-third, polarization (p. 224)
16. technology, political (p. 224)

PART VII: IN FOCUS—MAJOR ISSUES

1. Define each of the following, providing three examples for each.
   A. High-income countries:

   B. Middle-income countries:

   C. Low-income countries:

2. The authors of the text suggest that poverty in low-income countries is *more severe* and *more extensive* than in high-income countries. What evidence supports this statement?
   A. Severe:

   B. Extensive:

3. Identify and illustrate the six *correlates of global poverty*.

4. What is *modernization theory*?

5. What are the four stages in W.W. Rostow's theory of modernization?

6. According to modernization theory, what are the four roles played by high-income nations in global economic development?

7. What are five *criticisms* of modernization theory?

8. What is *dependency theory*?

9. Immanuel Wallerstein's dependency theory involves what three factors?

10. According to dependency theory, what is the role of high-income nations in world economic development?

11. What are five *criticisms* of dependency theory?

PART VIII: ANALYSIS AND COMMENT

Window on the World - Global Map 9-1
"Median Age at Death in Global Perspective"
Key Points: Questions:

Global Sociology
"God Made Me to Be a Slave"
Key Points: Questions:

Global Sociology
"A Different Kind of Poverty: A Report from India"
Key Points: Questions:

Social Diversity
"Modernization: New Challenges for Women"
Key Points: Questions:

Window on the World-Global Map 9-2
"Prosperity and Stagnation in Global Perspective"
Key Points: Questions:

Controversy and Debate
"Will the World Starve?"
Key Points: Questions:

Gender Stratification

10

PART I: CHAPTER OUTLINE
1. Gender and Inequality
    A. Male-Female Differences
    B. Patriarchy and Sexism
2. Gender and Socialization
    A. Gender and the Family
    B. Gender and the Peer Group
    C. Gender and Schooling
    D. Gender and the Mass Media
3. Gender and Social Stratification
    A. Working Women and Men
    B. Housework: Women's "Second Shift"
    C. Gender, Income, and Wealth
    D. Gender and Education
    E. Gender and Politics
    F. Are Women A Minority?
    G. Minority Women
    H. Violence Against Women
4. Theoretical Analysis of Gender
    A. Structural-Functional Analysis
    B. Social-Conflict Analysis
5. Feminism
    A. Basic Feminist Ideas
    B. Types of Feminism
    C. Opposition to Feminism
6. Looking Ahead: Gender in the Twenty-First Century
7. Summary
8. Key Concepts
9. Critical-Thinking Questions
10. Applications and Exercises
11. Sites to See

PART II: LEARNING OBJECTIVES

1. To know the distinction between male-female differences and gender stratification.
2. To become aware of the various types of social organizations found globally based upon the relationship between females and males.
3. To be able to describe the link between patriarchy and sexism, and to see how the nature of each is changing in modern society.
4. To be able to describe the role that gender plays in socialization in the family, the peer group, schooling, the mass media, and adult interaction.
5. To see how gender stratification occurs in the work world, education, and politics.
6. To consider key arguments in the debate over whether women constitute a minority.
7. To consider how the structural-functional and social-conflict paradigms help explain the origins and persistence of gender inequality.
8. To begin to recognize the extent to which women are victims of violence, and to begin to understand what we can do to change this problem.
9. To consider the central ideas of feminism, the variations of feminism, and resistance to feminism.

PART III: KEY CONCEPTS

feminism

gender

gender roles

gender stratification

matriarchy

minority

patriarchy

sexism

sexual harassment

PART IV: IMPORTANT RESEARCHERS

Margaret Mead

George Murdock

Talcott Parsons

Friedrich Engels

Janet Lever

Dorothy Smith

Carol Gilligan

PART V: STUDY QUESTIONS

True-False

1. T F *Gender* refers to the biological distinction between females and males.
2. T F *Gender stratification* is perhaps most clearly illustrated by the fact that men's life expectancy is greater than the life expectancy for women.
3. T F The experience of the *Israeli Kibbutzim* suggests that cultures have considerable latitude in defining what is masculine and feminine.
4. T F The conclusions made by *Margaret Mead* in her research on three New Guinea societies is consistent with the sociobiological argument that "persistent biological distinctions may undermine gender equality."
5. T F *George Murdock's* cross-cultural research has shown some general patterns in terms of which type of activities are classified as *masculine* or *feminine*; however, beyond this general pattern, significant variation exists.
6. T F Globally, *hunting* and *warfare* generally fall to men, while home-centred tasks such as cooking and child care generally fall to women.
7. T F In global perspective, societies consistently define only a few specific activities as *feminine* or *masculine*.
8. T F *Patriarchy* is a form of social organization in which males dominate females.
9. T F Research suggests that the vast majority of young people in Canada develop consistently "masculine" or "feminine" personalities.
10. T F Janet Lever's research on *play* suggests that boys favour team sports with complex rules and clear objectives.

11. T F Carol Gilligan's research on patterns of moral reasoning suggests that boys learn to reason according to "rules and principles" more than girls.
12. T F In 1999, more than half of all women over age 15 worked for income.
13. T F About a third of all women with children under age 3 work for income.
14. T F According to Naomi Wolf, the *beauty myth* arises, first, because society teaches women to measure themselves in terms of physical appearance, with standards that are unattainable.
15. T F Women make up about 30 percent of the *paid labour force*.
16. T F With women's entry into the labour force, the amount of *housework* performed by women has declined, but the share women do has stayed about the same.
17. T F for every dollar earned by men, women earn 72.5 cents.
18. T F At age forty, ninety percent of men, but only thirty-five percent of women in executive positions have at least one child.
19. T F Today, over one-half of all bachelor's degrees are earned by *women*.
20. T F Nowhere in the world do women hold more than one third of elected parliamentary seats.
21. T F According to the definition given in the text, *sexual harassment* always involves physical contact.
22. T F According to structural-functionalist Talcott Parsons, gender, at least in the traditional sense, forms a *complementary* set of roles that links men and women together.
23. T F Agrarian societies are typically less patriarchal than industrial societies.
24. T F *Liberal feminists* feel that individuals should be free to develop their own abilities and talents.

Multiple Choice

1. The personal traits and social positions that members of a society attach to being female and male refers to
   a) gender.
   b) sex.
   c) sexual orientation.
   d) gender stratification.

2. The unequal distribution of wealth, power, and privilege between men and women refers to
   a) secondary sex characteristics.
   b) gender division.
   c) gender stratification.
   d) gender discrimination.
   e) sexual orientation.

3. Which of the following has been found to be *true* about men and women?
   a) Global data show their average weights to be about the same.
   b) There are no overall differences in intelligence between males and females.
   c) Women marathon runners have not caught up to the fastest men of decades past.
   d) Global data show their average longevity is about the same.

4. Investigations of the *Israeli Kibbutzim* have indicated
   a) they are collective settlements.
   b) their members historically have embraced social equality.
   c) they support evidence of wide cultural latitude in defining what is feminine and masculine.
   d) men and women living there share both work and decision making.
   e) all of the above

5. The social inequality of men and women has been shown to be culturally based rather than exclusively biological by which of the following studies?
   a) Murdock's study of pre-industrial societies
   b) Israeli kibbutzim studies
   c) New Guinea studies by Margaret Mead
   d) all of the above

6. Margaret Mead's research on gender in three societies in New Guinea illustrates that
   a) diffusion tends to standardize gender role assignments for women and men.
   b) gender is primarily biologically determined.
   c) gender is treated virtually the same across societies.
   d) gender is a variable creation of culture.
   e) while gender roles vary cross-culturally for men, they are very consistent for women.

7. Among the *Mundugumor*, Margaret Mead found
   a) both females and males to be very passive.
   b) both males and females to be aggressive and selfish.
   c) females to be very aggressive and males to be passive.
   d) sex roles to be very similar to what they are in Canada.

8. A form of social organization in which females are dominated by males is termed
   a) matriarchy.
   b) oligarchy.
   c) patriarchy.
   d) egalitarian.

9. The belief that one sex is innately superior to the other refers to
   a) homophobia.
   b) heterosexism.
   c) sexism.
   d) sexual individualism.

10. _____ is/are attitudes and activities that a society links to each sex.
    a) Gender roles
    b) Sexual orientation
    c) Gender stratification
    d) Gender identity

11. Which of the following words is traditionally seen as applying to men?
    a) receptive
    b) analytical
    c) intuitive
    d) content
    e) cooperative

12. Research by Carol Gilligan and Janet Lever demonstrates the influence of _____ on gender roles.
    a) the peer group
    b) biology
    c) religion
    d) personality

13. Which of the following statements about women in the labour force is *inaccurate*?
    a) Most women are in the labour force.
    b) Most married women are in the paid labour force.
    c) Most women with children under the age of six are in the paid labour force.
    d) Less than half of all women with children under the age of three are in the paid labour force.

14. What percentage of *married and common-law couples* in Canada today count on two incomes?
    a) 51
    b) 61
    c) 71
    d) 81

15. On average, what percentage of a male's income does a female earn?
    a) 42.5
    b) 52.5
    c) 62.5
    d) 72.5
    e) 82.5

16. The main reason women earn less than men is caused by their
    a) age.
    b) marital status.
    c) type of work.
    d) father's occupation.

17. In 2001, the number of women elected as provincial premiers or territorial leaders in Canada was:
    a) 0
    b) 1
    c) 2
    d) 3
    e) 4

18. As a woman, where are you most likely to suffer *physical violence*?
    a) at work
    b) at home
    c) among friends
    d) on the streets

19. Many feminists want our society to use a(n) _____ standard when measuring for *sexual harassment*.
    a) effect
    b) intention
    c) quid pro quo
    d) quid pro quid

20. *Talcott Parsons* argued that there are two *complementary role sets* which exist to link males and females together with social institutions. He called these
    a) rational and irrational.
    b) effective and affective.
    c) fundamental and secondary.
    d) residual and basic.
    e) instrumental and expressive.

21. Which theorist suggested that the male dominance over women was linked to technological advances which led to surpluses of valued resources?
    a) Talcott Parsons
    b) Erving Goffman
    c) Friedrich Engels
    d) Janet Lever

22. Which of the following nations has the highest rate of *contraception use* by women of childbearing age?
    a) Norway
    b) the United Kingdom
    c) the United States
    d) Ireland

23. Which of the following is *not* a type of *feminism*?
    a) liberal
    b) socialist
    c) radical
    d) expressive

24. What variant of feminism links the social disadvantage of women primarily to the *capitalist economic system*?
   a) socialist
   b) expressive
   c) communal
   d) liberal

Matching

1. _____ The personal traits and social positions that members of a society attach to being female and male.
2. _____ The unequal distribution of wealth, power, and privilege between men and women.
3. _____ Did groundbreaking research on gender in New Guinea.
4. _____ A form of social organization in which females dominate males.
5. _____ The belief that one sex is innately superior to the other.
6. _____ Attitudes and activities that a society links to each sex.
7. _____ After spending a year watching children at play, concluded that boys favour team sports with complex rules and clear objectives.
8. _____ Any category of people, distinguished by physical or cultural difference, that is socially disadvantaged.
9. _____ Comments, gestures, or physical contact of a sexual nature that are deliberate, repeated, and unwelcome.
10. _____ A structural-functionalist, differentiated between instrumental and expressive roles.
11. _____ Argued that capitalism intensifies male dominance.
12. _____ The advocacy of social equality for the men and women in opposition to patriarchy and sexism.

a. matriarchy
b. feminism
c. Friedrich Engels
d. Janet Lever
e. gender stratification
f. sexism
g. gender
h. sexual harassment
i. a minority
j. gender roles
k. Talcott Parsons
l. Margaret Mead

Fill-in-the-blank

1. According to research cited in the text, adolescent males exhibit greater _____ ability, while adolescent females excel in _____ skills.

2. _____ are collective Jewish settlements in Israel in which remarkable strides have been made in social equality between women and men.

Study Guide

3. In her research on gender roles, Margaret Mead focussed on three New Guinea societies, the _____, _____, and the _____.

4. _____ is the belief that one sex is innately superior to the other.

5. _____ _____ are attitudes and activities that a society links to each sex.

6. Today in Canada, _____ percent of *women with children under the age of three* are in the labour force.

7. Since 1976, the labour force participation of men has _____ while that of women has _____.

8. Canadian women now make up _____ percent of all self-employed workers in Canada.

9. With women's entry into the labour force, the amount of *housework* performed by women has declined, but the _____ women do has stayed about the same.

10. The main reason women earn less than men is the _____ of work they do.

11. A _____ is any category of people, distinguished by physical or cultural difference, that is socially disadvantaged.

12. The two types of *violence* against women focussed on in the text include _____ _____ and _____.

13. _____ _____ refers to comments, gestures, or physical contact of a sexual nature that is deliberate, repeated, and unwelcome.

14. Talcott Parsons identified two *complementary roles* that link men and women. These include the _____ and _____.

15. _____ refers to the advocacy of social equality for men and women, in opposition to patriarchy and sexism.

16. Basic *feminist ideas* include the importance of _____, the expanding human _____, eliminating gender _____, ending sexual _____, and promoting sexual _____.

17. The three types of *feminism* are _____, _____, and _____.

Definition and Short-Answer

1. Briefly review the significant events in the history of the *Women's Movement* during the nineteenth century.
2. Compare the research by *Margaret Mead* in New Guinea with the research done at the Israeli *Kibbutzim* in terms of the cultural variability of gender roles.
3. What generalizations about the linkage between *sex* and *gender* can be made based on the cross-cultural research of *George Murdock*?
4. According to the authors, is *patriarchy* inevitable? Why? What roles have technological advances and industrialization played in the changes in the relative statuses of women and men in society?
5. *Table 10-1* presents lists of traits linked to the traditional gender identities of *femininity* and *masculinity*. Develop a questionnaire using the traits identified in this table to survey females and males to determine to what extent these traits differentiate between the sexes.
6. Identify five important points about *gender stratification* within the occupational domain of our society.
7. What are the explanations as to why males dominate *politics*? To what extent are the roles of women changing in this sphere of social life? What factors are influencing these changes?
8. Review the issue of *violence against women* in our society. What are the types of violence discussed? What are the demographics of violence?
9. Are women a *minority group*? What are the arguments for and against this idea? What is the evidence being presented in the Controversy and Debate box at the end of the chapter to suggest men may be a minority group?
10. Compare the analyses of gender stratification as provided through the *structural-functional* and *social-conflict* paradigms.
11. What are the five *basic principles* of *feminism*? Discuss the specific examples for each.
12. What are the three types of *feminism*? Briefly differentiate between them in terms of the basic arguments being made about gender roles in society.
13. What are the three general criticisms of the conclusions being made by *social-conflict* theorists concerning gender stratification?

14. What evidence can you provide from your own experience and observations concerning the argument being made by *Jessie Bernard* about the *pink* and *blue* worlds?

PART VI: ANSWERS TO STUDY QUESTIONS

True-False
1. F (p. 231)
2. F (p. 232)
3. T (p. 232)
4. F (pp.232-233)
5. T (p. 233)
6. T (p. 233)
7. F (p. 233)
8. T (p. 233)
9. F (p. 235)
10. T (p. 236)
11. T (p. 236)
12. T (pp.236-237)
13. F (p. 237)
14. T (p. 237)
15. F (p. 237)
16. T (p. 238)
17. T (p. 239)
18. T (p. 241)
19. T (p. 242)
20. F (p. 242)
21. F (p. 244)
22. T (p. 246)
23. F (p. 247)
24. T (p. 248)

Multiple-Choice
1. a (p. 231)
2. c (p. 232)
3. b (p. 232)
4. e (p. 232)
5. d (p. 232-233)
6. d (pp.232-233)
7. b (p. 233)
8. c (p. 233)
9. c (p. 234)
10. a (p. 235)
11. b (p. 235)
12. a (p. 236)
13. d (p. 237)
14. b (p. 237)
15. d (p. 239)
16. c (p. 239)
17. a (p. 242)
18. b (p. 244)
19. a (p. 244)
20. e (p. 246)
21. c (p. 246)
22. b (p. 248)
23. d (p. 248)
24. a (p. 248)

Matching
1. g (p. 231)
2. e (p. 232)
3. l (p. 233)
4. a (p. 233)
5. f (p. 234)
6. j (p. 235)
7. d (p. 236)
8. i (p. 243)
9. h (p. 244)
10. k (p. 246)
11. c (p. 247)
12. b (p. 247)

Fill-in-the-blank
1. mathematical, verbal (p. 232)
2. Kibbutzim (p. 232)
3. Arapesh, Mundugumor, Tchambuli (p. 233)
4. Sexism (p. 234)
5. Gender roles (p. 235)
6. 61 (p. 237)
7. decreased, increased (p. 238)
8. 35 (p. 238)
9. share (p. 238)
10. kind (type) (p. 239)
11. minority (p. 234)
12. Sexual harassment, pornography (pp. 244-245)
13. Sexual harassment (p. 244)
14. instrumental, expressive (p. 246)
15. Feminism (p. 247)
16. change, choice, stratification, violence, freedom (pp. 247-248)
17. liberal, socialist, radical (p. 265)

Society: The Basics, Second Canadian Edition

PART VII: IN FOCUS – IMPORTANT ISSUES

1. What does *Figure 10-1* indicate about the biological differences between females and males?

2. What are the significant biological differences between females and males?

3. What conclusions do you make when weighing the evidence presented by Margaret Mead and George Murdock concerning cross-cultural patterns of *gender roles*?

4. What are three *costs of sexism*?

5. Provide one illustration from the text concerning each of the following influences on *gender role socialization*.
    A. the family

    B. the peer group

    C. schooling

D. the mass media

6. Identify the percentages of employed people for each of the following categories:
    A. males (over 15): _____ (approximately)
    B. females (over 15): _____
    C. women with children under the age of six: _____
    D. women with children under the age of three: _____

7. What does *Figure 10-2* tell us? Why do you think these changes in labour force participation rates have occurred?

8. How does employment status affect women's *housework* labour? How about marital status? Presence of children? What about for men?

9. What is the factor that most influences the differences in pay for women and men?

10. Are women a *minority group*? Why?

11. How is *sexual harassment* defined?

12. How is *pornography* defined?

13. In what ways do sexual harassment and pornography represent *violence against women*?

14. Briefly discuss how each of the following theoretical paradigms views the issue of gender in society:
    A. structural-functionalist

    B. social-conflict

15. What are the four basic *feminist ideas* identified in the text?

16. Describe each of the following *types of feminism*:
    A. liberal

    B. socialist

C. radical

17. Why is there *opposition to feminism*?

18. What is the vision offered by the authors concerning the role of gender in society over the next century?

PART VIII: ANALYSIS AND COMMENT

Window on the World–Global Map 10-1
"Women's Power in Global Perspective"
Key Points: Questions:

Social Diversity
"Pretty Is as Pretty Does: The Beauty Myth"
Key Points: Questions:

Window on the World – Global Map 10-2
"Women's Paid Employment in Global Perspective"
Key Points: Questions:

Seeing Ourselves – National Map 10-1
"Labour Force Participation for Females over Age 15 Years with Children under Age 6 Years, Canada, 1996"
Key Points: Questions:

Controversy and Debate
"Men's Rights! Are Men Really So Privileged?"
Key Points: Questions:

Race and Ethnicity

PART I: CHAPTER OUTLINE
1. The Social Meaning of Race and Ethnicity
    A. Race
    B. Ethnicity
    C. Minorities
    D. Prejudice and Stereotypes
    E. Racism
    F. Theories of Prejudice
    G. Discrimination
    H. Institutional Prejudice and Discrimination
    I. Prejudice and Discrimination: The Vicious Circle
2. Majority and Minority: Patterns of Interaction
    A. Pluralism
    B. Assimilation
    C. Segregation
    D. Genocide
3. Race and Ethnicity in Canada
    A. Canada's Aboriginal Peoples
    B. British Canadians
    C. French Canadians
    D. Canada's other Immigrants
    E. Visible Minorities
4. Looking Ahead: Race and Ethnicity
5. Summary
6. Key Concepts
7. Critical-Thinking Questions
8. Applications and Exercises
9. Sites to See

PART II: LEARNING OBJECTIVES

1. To develop an understanding about the biological basis for definitions of race.
2. To be able to distinguish between the biological concept of race and the cultural concept of ethnicity.
3. To be able to identify the characteristics of a minority group.
4. To be able to identify and describe prejudice.
5. To be able to identify and describe four theories of prejudice.
6. To be able to distinguish between prejudice and discrimination.
7. To be able to provide examples of institutional prejudice and discrimination.
8. To be able to see how prejudice and discrimination combine to create a vicious circle.
9. To be able to describe the patterns of interaction between minorities and the majority.
10. To be able to describe the histories and relative statuses of each of the groups identified in the text.

PART III: KEY CONCEPTS

assimilation

discrimination

ethnicity

genocide

institutional prejudice and discrimination

miscegenation

pluralism

race

racism

scapegoat

segregation

PART IV: IMPORTANT RESEARCHERS

Robert Merton   Emory Bogardus

T. W. Adorno   Thomas Sowell

PART V: STUDY QUESTIONS

True-False

1. T F Physical diversity appeared among our human ancestors as the result of living in different *geographic regions* of the word.
2. T F Although *racial categories* point to some biological elements, *race* is a socially constructed concept.
3. T F According to the authors of our text, for sociological purposes the concepts of *race* and *ethnicity* can be used interchangeably.
4. T F A racial or ethnic *minority* is a category of people, distinguished by physical or cultural traits, who are socially disadvantaged.
5. T F Ethnicity involves *even more variability* than race.
6. T F The *scapegoat theory* links prejudice to frustration and suggests that prejudice is likely to be pronounced among people who themselves are disadvantaged.
7. T F Emory Bogardus' concept of *social distance* is used in the *cultural theory* of prejudice, which suggests that some prejudice is found in everyone because it is embedded in culture.
8. T F Thomas Sowell has argued that *IQ* is directly related to biological forces, citing the great stability in average IQ scores for different categories of racial and ethnic groups.
9. T F In *Robert Merton's* typology of patterns of prejudice and discrimination, an unprejudiced-nondiscriminator is labelled an "all-weather liberal."
10. T F According to the authors, as a cultural process, *assimilation* involves changes in ethnicity but not in race.
11. T F Visible minorities tend to live in specific areas of our cities.
12. T F *Genocide* is the systematic annihilation of one category of people by another.
13. T F There are several recent examples of genocide.
14. T F The first Europeans were decimated by *virgin soil epidemics* after arriving to North America.
15. T F Aboriginals in Canada were not entitled to vote until 1910.
16. T F More than 1 million Canadians claim some Aboriginal ancestry.
17. T F About five million claimed exclusively British ancestry in the 1996 census.
18. T F Bill 101 gives equal rights to all languages.

19. T F In 1920 schooling in British Columbia was integrated by legislation.
20. T F Almost one in five people in Canada were born outside of Canada.
21. T F On average, visible minorities have more education and a higher income than other Canadians.
22. T F Prejudice and discrimination towards immigrants have decreased recently.

Multiple Choice

1. Which of the following is *not* true about the residential school system for Aboriginals described in the opening vignette?
   a) Children were separated from their parents by physical force if parents objected.
   b) It was abolished by the Indian Act of 1874.
   c) Education authorities were federally appointed.
   d) Successful graduates were still excluded from mainstream society.
   e) Once they returned, many educated Aboriginals found it hard to accept the teachings of their elders.

2. A socially constructed category composed of people who share biologically transmitted traits that members of a society deem socially significant is the definition for
   a) race.
   b) minority group.
   c) ethnicity.
   d) assimilation.

3. A shared cultural heritage is the definition for
   a) a minority group.
   b) race.
   c) ethnicity.
   d) assimilation.
   e) pluralism.

4. Among people of *European descent,* the largest number of people in Canada trace their ancestry back to
   a) Italy.
   b) Ireland.
   c) Germany.
   d) Russia.
   e) England.

5. Members of an *ethnic category* share
   a) common ancestors, language, and religion.
   b) only biological distinctions.
   c) residential location.
   d) social class ranking.
   e) none of the above.

6. There are _____ distinct ethnic categories in Canada.
   a) about 20
   b) about 40
   c) about 60
   d) about 80
   e) more than 100

7. *Minority groups* have two major characteristics:
   a) race and ethnicity.
   b) religion and ethnicity
   c) physical traits and political orientation.
   d) sexual orientation and race.
   e) distinctive identity and subordination.

8. What is the term for a category of people, set apart by physical or cultural traits, that is socially disadvantaged?
   a) minority group
   b) stereotype
   c) ethnicity
   d) race

9. What is the term for a rigid and irrational generalization about an entire category of people?
   a) racism
   b) discrimination
   c) stereotype
   d) prejudice

10. What is the term for a biased characterization of some category of people?
    a) racism
    b) stereotype
    c) discrimination
    d) prejudice

11. A *form of prejudice* referring to the belief that one racial category is innately superior or inferior to another is called
    a) stereotyping.
    b) discrimination.
    c) racism.
    d) scapegoating.

12. One explanation of the origin of prejudice is found in the concept of the *authoritarian personality*. Such a personality exhibits
    a) an attitude of authority over others believed to be inferior.
    b) frustration over personal troubles directed toward someone less powerful.
    c) rigid conformity to conventional cultural norms and values.
    d) social distance from others deemed inferior.

13. Treating various categories of people unequally refers to
    a) prejudice.
    b) stereotyping.
    c) miscegenation.
    d) discrimination.

14. *Robert Merton's* study of the relationship between prejudice and discrimination revealed one behavioural type that discriminates against persons even though he or she is not prejudiced. This person would be called a(n)
    a) active bigot.
    b) all-weather liberal.
    c) timid bigot.
    d) fair-weather liberal.

15. According to the work of W. I. Thomas, a *vicious circle* is formed by which variables?
    a) miscegenation and authoritarianism
    b) race and ethnicity
    c) pluralism and assimilation
    d) segregation and integration
    e) prejudice and discrimination

16. A state in which racial and ethnic minorities are distinct but have social parity is termed
    a) segregation.
    b) pluralism.
    c) integration.
    d) assimilation.

17. *Pluralism* has only limited application Canadian society because
    a) most Canadians only want to maintain their distinctive identities to a point.
    b) our society's tolerance for diversity is limited.
    c) people of different colours and cultures don't have equal standing.
    d) all of the above

18. The process by which minorities gradually adopt patterns of the dominant culture is known as
    a) pluralism.
    b) amalgamation.
    c) assimilation.
    d) miscegenation.

19. *Miscegenation* is
    a) the biological reproduction by partners of different racial categories.
    b) the process by which minorities gradually adopt patterns of the dominant culture.
    c) a state in which all categories of people are distinct but have social parity.
    d) a condition of prejudice leading to discrimination.

20. Which of the following groups are the least dispersed in our cities?
    a) British
    b) French
    c) Visible Minorities
    d) Germans

21. Which of the following is *not true* about Aboriginals in Canada?
    a) Aboriginals earn below the average income for Canadians.
    b) Aboriginals have higher rates of unemployment than other Canadians.
    c) Aboriginals are more likely to live in single-parent families than other Canadians.
    d) Aboriginals have higher rates of tuberculosis than other Canadians.
    e) The size of the Aboriginal population is declining.

22. Which of the following statements is/are accurate concerning *white Anglo Saxon Protestants (WASPs)?*
    a) They represent more than 16 percent of our nation's population.
    b) Historically, WASP immigrants were highly skilled and motivated to achieve by what we now call the Protestant work ethic.
    c) WASPs were never one single social group.
    d) The English language dominates our media.
    e) All of the above are accurate statements about WASPs.

23. When the French immigrated in the 17th century they were going to a place called
    a) the Old World.
    b) British North America.
    c) Quebec.
    d) New France.

24. The Quebec referendum on separation that saw less than one percent of votes separating Yes from No occurred in
    a) 1955.
    b) 1965.
    c) 1975.
    d) 1985.
    e) 1995.

25. The largest group of immigrants that enter Canada today are
    a) Northern European.
    b) American.
    c) English.
    d) French.
    e) visible minorities.

26. Which of the following is *not true* about the Nisga'a Treaty?
    a) Nisga'a are no longer Aboriginal peoples under the constitution.
    b) Federal and provincial laws no longer apply to Nisga'a people.
    c) Nisga'a people will still be exempt from sales and income tax.
    d) The Charter of Rights and Freedoms no longer applies to Nisga'a people.
    e) None of the above are true.

27. The largest visible minority group in Canada is
    a) South Asian.
    b) Chinese.
    c) Black.
    d) Arab/West Asian.
    e) Filipino.

28. Approximately how large is the Canadian visible minority population?
    a) 1 million
    b) 3 million
    c) 5 million
    d) 7 million
    e) 9 million

29. Among those who are employed on a full-year, full-time basis, the only group of visible minority women that earn more than other women are those aged
    a) 15-24.
    b) 25-44.
    c) 45-54.
    d) 55-64.
    e) 65 and over.

30. The largest concentration of immigrants can be found in
    a) rural areas.
    b) the far north.
    c) the Atlantic provinces.
    d) our largest cities.
    e) Quebec.

Matching

1. _____ A socially constructed category composed of people who share biologically transmitted traits that members of a society consider important.
2. _____ A shared cultural heritage.
3. _____ A category of people, distinguished by physical or cultural traits, that is socially disadvantaged.
4. _____ An approach contending that while extreme prejudice may characterize some people, some prejudice is found in everyone.
5. _____ A person or category of people, typically with little power, whom people unfairly blame for their troubles.
6. _____ A theory holding that prejudice springs from frustration among people who are themselves disadvantaged.
7. _____ A state in which racial and ethnic minorities are distinct but have social parity.
8. _____ The process by which minorities gradually adopt patterns of the dominant culture.
9. _____ Persons, other than Aboriginal peoples, who are non-Caucasian in race or non-white in colour.
10. _____ Hostility toward foreigners.

a. xenophobia
b. assimilation
c. minority
d. scapegoat
e. ethnicity
f. visible minorities
g. cultural theory
h. pluralism
i. race
j. scapegoat theory

Fill-in-the-blank

1. The term _____ refers to a socially constructed category composed of people who share biologically transmitted traits that members of society consider important.

2. The three-part scheme of racial classification developed by biologists during the nineteenth century included _____, _____, and _____.

3. While *race* is a _____ concept, *ethnicity* is a _____ concept.

4. Two major characteristics of *minorities* are that they have a _____ identity and are _____ by the social-stratification system.

5. A _____ refers to a rigid and irrational generalization about an entire category of people.

6. _____ *theory* holds that prejudice springs from frustration.

7. Thomas Sowell has demonstrated that most of the documented racial difference in intelligence is not due to _____ but to people's _____.

8. _____ prejudice or discrimination refers to bias in attitudes or actions inherent in the operation of any of society's institutions.

9. _____ is the process by which minorities gradually adopt patterns of the dominant culture.

10. _____ is the systematic killing of one category of people by another.

11. Not until _____ were Aboriginal Canadians entitled to vote.

12. The majority of those who consider themselves an Aboriginal person identify themselves as _____ _____ Indians, a minority declare themselves to be _____ and a smaller number still report _____ ancestry.

13. The 1996 census showed that even though only 5 percent of the Aboriginal population lived in the former _____ _____, a majority of the population there was Aboriginal.
14. The _____ tax on Chinese immigrants was $500 in 1904.
15. Those born in the United Kingdom, Italy and the United States make up _____ percent of the total population of Canadians born outside of Canada.
16. Visible minorities tend to have a _____ education and earn a _____ income than other Canadians.
17. About _____ in three visible minority persons are born in Canada.
18. Most immigrants to Canada today come from _____- and _____- income countries.

Short-Answer and Definition
1. Identify and describe the four *explanations* of why prejudice exists.
2. Differentiate between the concepts *prejudice* and *discrimination*.
3. What are the four types of people identified by *Robert Merton's* typology of patterns of prejudice and discrimination? Provide an illustration for each.
4. What is *institutional prejudice and discrimination*? Provide two illustrations.
5. What are the four models representing the *patterns of interaction* between minority groups and the majority group? Define and discuss an illustration for each of these.
6. How do Aboriginals and visible minorities compare to others in terms of relative social standing using the variables of *educational achievement, family income,* and *poverty rates*?
7. Review the history and current characteristics of segregation in Canada.
8. What were the most prominent examples of *genocide* in the 20th century?
9. Briefly discuss the history and causes of Aboriginal population change since the arrival of Europeans.
10. Discuss the relevance of the label "two solitudes" in contemporary Canada.
11. Briefly describe the changing characteristics of immigrants to Canada over time.
12. What are the characteristics of the Nisga'a treaty?
13. Differentiate between the concepts of *race* and *ethnicity*.
14. How are the changing patterns in *immigration* likely to influence the future of Canada?

PART VI: ANSWERS TO STUDY QUESTIONS

True-False
1. T (p. 256)
2. T (p. 256)
3. F (p. 258)
4. T (p. 258)
5. T (p. 258)
6. T (p. 260)
7. T (p. 261)
8. F (pp. 260-261)
9. T (p. 263)
10. T (p. 265)
11. T (p. 265)
12. T (p. 266)
13. T (p. 266)
14. F (p. 267)
15. F (p. 267)
16. T (p. 267)
17. T (p. 268)
18. F (p. 269)
19. F (p. 270)
20. T (p. 270)
21. F (p. 271)
22. F (p. 272)

Multiple Choice
1. b (p. 255)
2. a (p. 256)
3. c (p. 257)
4. e (p. 257)
5. a (p. 257)
6. e (p. 258)
7. e (p. 258)
8. a (p. 258)
9. d (p. 259)
10. b (p. 259)
11. c (p. 259)
12. c (p. 261)
13. d (p. 263)
14. d (p. 263)
15. e (p. 263)
16. b (p. 264)
17. d (pp. 264-265)
18. c (p. 265)
19. a (p. 265)
20. c (p. 265)
21. e (p. 267-268)
22. e (p. 268)
23. d (p. 268)
24. e (p. 269)
25. e (pp. 270-271)
26. e (pp. 270-271)
27. b (p. 272)
28. b (p. 272)
29. e (p. 272)
30. d (p. 273)

Matching
1. i (p. 256)
2. e (p. 257)
3. c (p. 258)
4. g (p. 261)
5. d (p. 260)
6. j (p. 260)
7. h (p. 269)
8. b (p. 265)
9. f (p. 271)
10. a (p. 272)

Fill-in-the-blank
1. race (p. 256)
2. Caucasian, Negroid, Mongoloid (p. 256)
3. biological, cultural (pp. 256-257)
4. distinctive, subordinated (p. 258)
5. prejudice (p. 259)
6. Scapegoat (p. 260)
7. biology, environments (p. 260-261)
8. institutional (p. 263)
9. assimilation (p. 265)
10. genocide (p. 266)
11. 1960 (p. 267)
12. North American, Métis, Inuit (p. 267)
13. Northwest Territories (p. 268)
14. head (p. 269)
15. 25 (p. 270)
16. higher, lower (p. 271)
17. one (p. 271)
18. middle, low (p. 272)

Society: The Basics, Second Canadian Edition

PART VII: IN FOCUS—IMPORTANT ISSUES

Regarding the *social meaning* of race and ethnicity, answer the following questions.

1. Differentiate between the concepts of *race* and *ethnicity*.

2. What do the authors mean by saying that ethnicity involves more *variability* than race?

3. What are the basic characteristics of a *minority group*?

4. How do the authors define *prejudice*?

5. Briefly describe each of the following *theories of prejudice*.
    A. Scapegoat Theory

    B. Authoritarian Personality Theory

C. Cultural Theory

D. Conflict Theory

6. How does discrimination differ from prejudice?

7. Provide two illustrations of *institutional discrimination*.

8. Provide an illustration for each of the four patterns of prejudice and discrimination as outlined by Robert Merton.

9. Define and illustrate each of the following *patterns of interaction* between racial and ethnic groups:
   A. Pluralism

   B. Assimilation

   C. Segregation

   D. Genocide

10. Identify three important characteristics for the following racial and ethnic groups that differentially characterize them in our society's social stratification system.
    A. Aboriginal Peoples

    B. British Canadians

    C. French Canadians

    D. Canada's Other Immigrants

E. Visible Minorities

11. What are the issues today that are different from those of the past concerning *immigration* to the Canada? What issues have not changed?

PART VIII: ANALYSIS AND COMMENT

Applying Sociology
"Does Race Affect Intelligence?"

Key Points: Questions:

Social Diversity
"Racism in Canada: Numbers and Places in the News"

Key Points: Questions:

Controversy and Debate
"Should Certain Groups in Canada Enjoy Special Rights?"

Key Points: Questions:

Seeing Ourselves National Map 11-1
"The Percentage of Immigrants, Visible Minorities, and Aboriginals by Census Division, Canada, 1996"

Key Points: Questions:

Economics and Politics

PART I: CHAPTER OUTLINE

1. The Economy: Historical Overview
    A. The Agricultural Revolution
    B. The Industrial Revolution
    C. The Information Revolution and the Post-Industrial Society
    D. Sectors of the Economy
    E. The Global Economy
2. Economic Systems: Paths to Justice
    A. Capitalism
    B. Socialism
    C. Welfare Capitalism and State Capitalism
    D. Relative Advantages of Capitalism and Socialism
    E. Changes in Socialist Countries
3. Work in the Post-Industrial Economy
    A. The Changing Workplace
    B. Labour Unions
    C. Professions
    D. Self-Employment
    E. Unemployment
    F. Workplace Diversity: Race and Gender
    G. New Information Technology and Work
4. Corporations
    A. Economic Concentration
    B. Corporate Linkages
    C. Corporations: Are They Competitive?
    D. Corporations and the Global Economy
    E. Looking Ahead: The Economy of the Twenty-First Century

5. Politics Historical Overview
6. Global Political Systems
    A. Monarchy
    B. Democracy
    C. Authoritarianism
    D. Totalitarianism
    E. A Global Political System?

7. Politics in Canada
    A. Canadian Culture and the Rise of the Welfare State
    B. The Political Spectrum
    C. Party Identification
    D. Special-Interest Groups
    E. Voter Apathy
8. Theoretical Analysis of Politics
    A. The Pluralist Model: The People Rule
    B. The Power-Elite Model: A Few People Rule
    C. The Marxist Model: Bias in the System Itself
9. Power Beyond the Rules
    A. Revolution
    B. Terrorism
10. War and Peace
    A. The Causes of War
    B. The Costs and Causes of Militarism
    C. Nuclear Weapons
    D. Pursuing of Peace
    E. Looking Ahead: Politics in the Twenty-First Century
11. Summary
    A. Economics
    B. Politics
12. Key Concepts
    A. Economics
    B. Politics
13. Critical-Thinking Questions
14. Applications and Exercises
15. Sites to See

PART II: LEARNING OBJECTIVES

1. To be able to identify the elements of the economy.
2. To be able to review the history and development of economic activity from the Agricultural Revolution through the Post-industrial Revolution.
3. To be able to identify and describe the three sectors of the economy.
4. To be able to compare the economic systems of capitalism, state capitalism, socialism, and democratic socialism.
5. To be able to explain the difference between socialism and communism.
6. To be able to describe the general characteristics and trends of work in the Canadian post-industrial society.
7. To begin to see the impact of multinational corporations on the world economy.
8. To recognize the difference between power and authority.
9. To be able to identify, define, and illustrate the different types of authority.
10. To be able to compare the four principal kinds of political systems.
11. To be able to describe the nature of the Canadian political system of government, and discuss the principal characteristics of the political spectrum of Canada.

12. To be able to compare the pluralist and power-elite models of political power.
13. To be able to describe the types of political power that exceed, or seek to eradicate, established politics.
14. To be able to identify the factors which increase the likelihood of war.
15. To recognize the historical pattern of militarism around the world, and to consider factors which can be used in the pursuit of peace.

PART III: KEY CONCEPTS

Economics:

capitalism

corporation

economy

global economy

monopoly

oligopoly

post-industrial economy

primary sector

profession

secondary sector

social institution

socialism

state capitalism

tertiary sector

welfare capitalism

Politics:

authoritarianism

authority

democracy

Society: The Basics, Second Canadian Edition

Marxist political-economy model

military-industrial complex

monarchy

pluralist model

political revolution

politics

power

power-elite model

routinization of charisma

terrorism

totalitarianism

war

welfare state

PART IV: IMPORTANT RESEARCHERS

Economics:
Karl Marx

Politics:

Max Weber	Wallace Clement
C. Wright Mills	Quincy Wright

PART V: STUDY QUESTIONS

True-False: Economics

1. T F The *economy* includes the production, distribution, and consumption of both goods and services.
2. T F *Agriculture*, as a subsistence strategy, first emerged some five thousand years ago.
3. T F The *primary sector* of the economy is the part of the economy that generates raw material directly from the natural environment.
4. T F The terms *primary, secondary,* and *tertiary,* referring to sectors of the economy, imply a ranking in importance for our society.
5. T F Agriculture occupies more than eighty percent of the labour force in *low-income countries.*
6. T F The largest economic sector of *middle-income countries* is the secondary sector.
7. T F *Socialism* is defined as both a political and economic system.
8. T F Per capita GDP tended to be significantly higher in capitalist as compared to socialist economies during the 1970s and 1980s.
9. T F *State capitalism* refers to an economic and political system in which companies are privately owned but cooperate closely with the government.
10. T F The *income ratio*, as a measure of the distribution of income in a society, tended to be higher in socialist systems as compared to capitalist systems during the 1970s and 1980s.
11. T F About 75 percent of employed men and women in Canada hold *service jobs*.
12. T F About 75 percent of Canadian workers belong to a labour union.
13. T F A larger percentage of workers today are *self-employed* than in any other period in the history of Canada.
14. T F Most *self-employed* people in Canada are in white-collar jobs.
15. T F According to the text, the Information Revolution is changing the kind of work people do and where they do it. Part of the consequence of this process is that computers are *de-skilling labour*.
16. T F More than 200 000 Canadians are self-employed and operate one or more corporations that do not have any employees.
17. T F The largest corporation in Canada in terms of sales is IBM.
18. T F An *oligopoly* refers to domination of a market by a few producers.

True-False: Politics

1. T F *Authority* is power people perceive as legitimate rather than coercive.
2. T F *Charismatic authority* is limited to the pre-industrialized world.
3. T F *Traditional authority* is sometimes referred to as *bureaucratic authority*.
4. T F *Authoritarianism* refers to a political system that denies popular participation in government.

5. T F In 1999, eighty-eight of the world's nations, containing forty percent of all people, were *politically free*—that is, they offered their citizens extensive political rights and civil liberties.

6. T F *Totalitarian* governments span the political spectrum from fascist to communist.

7. T F In Canada today, tax revenue, as a share of gross domestic product, is higher than in any other industrialized society.

8. T F Government benefits are so extensive in Canada that they begin even before birth.

9. T F Generally, the *New Democratic Party* supports more liberal policies regarding social and economic programs than does the *Canadian Alliance*.

10. T F Party identification is strong in Canada.

11. T F Special-interest groups campaign along party lines.

12. T F *Voter apathy* is a problem, as evidenced by the fact that citizens today are less likely to vote than were citizens a century ago.

13. T F High-income people are more likely to vote than are low-income people.

14. T F According to the *pluralist model* of Canadian politics, we are a democracy in which power is widely dispersed.

15. T F Research by Wallace Clement supported the *pluralist model* concerning how power is distributed in Canada.

16. T F One of the four insights offered concerning *terrorism* is that democracies are especially vulnerable to it because these governments afford extensive civil liberties to their people and have limited police networks.

17. T F The world's nations spend about $16 for every person on the planet for military purposes.

18. T F In recent years, defence has been the largest single expenditure by the U.S. government (16 percent of total spending in 1999).

19. T F The *military-industrial complex* refers to the close association of the federal government, the military, and defence industries.

20. T F It is estimated that by 2010 about five nations will have the ability to fight a *nuclear war*.

Multiple Choice: Economics

1. Which of the following is not a way in which *industrialization* changed the economy?
   a) new forms of energy
   b) centralization of work into factories
   c) manufacturing and mass production
   d) generalization
   e) wage labour

2. A productive system based on service work and extensive use of information technology refers to
   a) the post-industrial economy.
   b) the primary sector.
   c) the secondary sector.
   d) a cottage industry.

3. The *sector* of the economy that transforms raw materials into manufactured goods is termed the
   a) primary sector.
   b) competitive sector.
   c) secondary sector.
   d) basic sector.
   e) manifest sector.

4. Which of the following is *not a sector* of the modern economy?
   a) primary
   b) manifest
   c) secondary
   d) tertiary

5. Your occupation is teaching. In what production *sector* of the economy do you work?
   a) primary
   b) secondary
   c) tertiary
   d) manifest

6. You mine gold for a living. In what production *sector* of the economy do you work?
   a) tertiary
   b) manifest
   c) secondary
   d) auxiliary
   e) primary

7. Today, about _____ percent of the Canadian labour force is in *service work*, including secretarial and clerical work and positions in food service, sales, law, advertising, and teaching.
   a) 98
   b) 88
   c) 75
   d) 60
   e) 52

8. What is the *economic system* in which natural resources and the means of producing goods and services are privately owned?
   a) capitalism
   b) socialism
   c) communism
   d) state capitalism

9. Which of the following is/are accurate statements concerning *capitalism*?
   a) Justice, in a capitalist context, amounts to freedom of the marketplace where one can produce, invest, and buy according to individual self-interest.
   b) A purely capitalist economy is a free-market system with no government interference, sometimes called a laissez-faire economy.
   c) Consumers regulate a free-market economy.
   d) All are accurate statements concerning capitalism.

10. Which of the following is/are accurate statements concerning *socialism*?
    a) Socialism is characterized by collective ownership of property.
    b) Socialism rejects the laissez-faire approach.
    c) Justice, in a socialist context, is not freedom to compete and accumulate wealth but, rather, meeting everyone's basic needs in a more or less equal manner.
    d) All of the above are accurate statements concerning socialism.

11. Sweden and Italy represent what type of economic and political system?
    a) capitalism
    b) socialism
    c) communism
    d) welfare capitalism

12. An economic and political system that combines a mostly market-based economy with extensive social-welfare programs is termed
    a) socialism.
    b) market socialism.
    c) market communism.
    d) an oligarchy.
    e) welfare capitalism.

13. An economic and political system in which companies are privately owned although they cooperate closely with the government is known as
    a) state socialism.
    b) state capitalism.
    c) welfare capitalism.
    d) communism.

14. *Capitalist* economies had about _____ times the per capita GDP during the 1980s as *socialist* economies.
    a) 2.7
    b) 12.9
    c) 8.2
    d) .75
    e) 1.3

15. During the 1970s and 1980s, *socialist economies* had about _____ as much *income inequality* as was found in capitalist economies during the same time period.
    a) one-tenth
    b) one-half
    c) twice
    d) three times
    e) four times

Study Guide

16. Which of the following statements is/are *accurate*?
    a) Capitalist economies support a higher overall standard of living than socialist economies, with greater income disparity.
    b) Socialist economies create more economic equality than capitalist economies, but with a lower overall standard of living.
    c) Capitalism emphases freedom to pursue one's own self-interest.
    d) Socialism emphases freedom from basic want.
    e) All of the above.

17. What percentage of women in Canada had *income-producing jobs* in 1999?
    a) 31.7
    b) 23.5
    c) 44.6
    d) 81.5
    e) 54.6

18. By 2000, _____ percent of *new jobs* were in the *service sector*.
    a) 50
    b) 60
    c) 70
    d) 80
    e) 90

19. Today in Canada, 4 percent of the labour force is engaged in the primary sector. In 1911 the figure was
    a) 10 percent.
    b) 25 percent.
    c) 40 percent.
    d) 55 percent.

20. Today, _____ percent of the total employed workforce in Canada is *unionized*.
    a) over 40
    b) 32
    c) 22
    d) 16
    e) less than 10

21. A _____ is a prestigious, white-collar occupation that requires extensive formal education.
    a) profession
    b) career
    c) technical occupation
    d) primary sector work

22. Currently, about what percentage of the Canadian labour force is *self-employed*?
    a) less than 1
    b) 9
    c) 17
    d) 25
    e) 33

23. Which of the following statements is *most accurate*?
    a) Visible minority and Aboriginal men have a much higher rate of unemployment than visible minority and Aboriginal women.
    b) A much higher proportion of Aboriginal women are unemployed than Aboriginal men.
    c) Aboriginals have a lower unemployment rate than visible minorities.
    d) Visible minority women have a lower unemployment rate than visible minority men.
    e) Non-visible minority women have a lower unemployment rate than visible minority and Aboriginal men.

24. The *Information Revolution* is changing the nature of work in our society in which of the following ways?
    a) Computer are "deskilling" labour.
    b) Computers are making work more abstract.
    c) Computers limit workplace interaction.
    d) Computers increase employer's control of workers.
    e) All of the above.

25. What is the term for an organization with legal existence, including rights and liabilities, apart from those of its members?
    a) corporation
    b) bureaucracy
    c) business
    d) conglomerate

26. What is the term for giant corporations composed of many smaller corporations?
    a) megacorporations
    b) monopolies
    c) multinational corporations
    d) conglomerates
    e) oligarchies

27. Which Canadian corporation leads the nation in sales?
    a) IBM
    b) General Motors
    c) Suncor
    d) Trans Canada Pipelines
    e) Alcan

28. What is the term for a social network made up of people who simultaneously serve on the board of directors of many corporations?
    a) conglomerate
    b) interlocking directorate
    c) oligopoly
    d) monopoly

29. The domination of a market by a single producer is called a(n)
    a) conglomerate.
    b) interlocking directorate.
    c) monopoly.
    d) oligopoly.

30. In 1998, the average *hourly wage* for a Canadian worker in manufacturing was US$13.09. At over US$19.00 per hour, which country had the highest average wage for working in the manufacturing sector?
   a) France
   b) Russia
   c) Germany
   d) South Korea

Multiple Choice: Politics

1. Who defined *power* as the ability to achieve desired ends despite resistance?
   a) C. Wright Mills
   b) Max Weber
   c) Alexis de Tocqueville
   d) Robert Lynd

2. Power that people perceive as being *legitimate* rather than coercive is the definition for
   a) a monarchy.
   b) totalitarianism.
   c) government.
   d) politics.
   e) authority.

3. Which of the following is *not* one of the general contexts in which power is commonly defined as authority?
   a) traditional
   b) charismatic
   c) rational-legal
   d) democratic

4. Power that is legitimated by respect for long-established cultural patterns is called
   a) traditional.
   b) sacred.
   c) political.
   d) charismatic.
   e) power-elite.

5. According to *Max Weber*, the survival of a charismatic movement depends upon
   a) pluralism.
   b) political action.
   c) routinization.
   d) assimilation.

6. Norway, Spain, Belgium, Great Britain, the Netherlands, and Denmark are all contemporary examples of what form of government?
   a) totalitarian democracies
   b) authoritarian
   c) constitutional monarchies
   d) absolute monarchies
   e) communist democracies

Society: The Basics, Second Canadian Edition

7. What percentage of humanity lives in nations that are classified as being *free*, with considerable respect for civil liberties?
   a) 14
   b) 21
   c) 40
   d) 62
   e) 50

8. _____ refers to a highly centralized political system that extensively regulates people's lives.
   a) Authoritarianism
   b) Totalitarianism
   c) Absolute monarchy
   d) State capitalism

9. Relatively speaking, which of the following nations has the largest government, based on tax revenues as a share of gross national product?
   a) Japan
   b) France
   c) the United States
   d) Canada
   e) Sweden

10. A _____ refers to a range of government agencies and programs that provides benefits to the population.
    a) socialist system
    b) democracy
    c) authoritarian government
    d) welfare state
    e) political spectrum

11. In 2000-2001 the Canadian federal budget amounted to
    a) $16.2 billion
    b) $162 billion
    c) $1.62 trillion
    d) $16.2 trillion

12. In making sense of people's *political attitudes*, analysts distinguish between two kinds of issue, including
    a) institutional and personal.
    b) economic and social.
    c) structural and moral.
    d) national and international.

13. Since 1993 only one political party in Canada has consistently enjoyed more popular support than the other parties. That party is the
    a) Alliance
    b) Conservatives
    c) BQ
    d) Liberals
    e) NDP

14. Which of the following statements is/are accurate concerning *voting* in the United States?
    a) Seniors are more likely to vote than young people.
    b) A smaller and smaller share of eligible citizens actually do vote.
    c) Women are less likely to vote than men.
    d) Aboriginals are less likely to vote than visible minorities.
    e) All of the above are accurate statements.

15. Which idea below represents the *pluralist model* of power?
    a) Power is highly concentrated.
    b) Voting cannot create significant political changes.
    c) The Canadian power system is an oligarchy.
    d) Power is widely dispersed throughout society.

16. With which general sociological paradigm is the *power-elite model* associated?
    a) social-conflict
    b) symbolic-interaction
    c) structural-functional
    d) social-exchange

17. An analysis that explains politics in terms of the operation of society's *economic system* is referred to as
    a) pluralist theory.
    b) Marxist political-economy model.
    c) power-elite model.
    d) welfare state model.

18. Researchers using the _____ view voter apathy as *indifference*.
    a) power-elite model
    b) liberal-democratic model
    c) pluralist model
    d) Marxist model

19. In which stage of *revolution* does the danger of counterrevolution occur?
    a) rising expectations
    b) unresponsive government
    c) establishing a new legitimacy
    d) radical leadership by intellectuals

20. According to Paul Johnson, which of the following is/are distinguishing characteristics of *terrorism*?
    a) Terrorists try to paint violence as a legitimate political tactic.
    b) Terrorism is employed not just by groups, but by governments against their own people.
    c) Democratic societies reject terrorism in principle, but they are especially vulnerable to terrorists because they afford extensive civil liberties.
    d) Terrorism is always a matter of definition.
    e) all of the above

21. *Quincy Wright* has identified several circumstances as conditions which lead humans to go to war. Which of the following is *not* one of these?
    a) perceived threat
    b) political objectives
    c) social problems
    d) moral objectives
    e) wide-ranging alternatives

22. Together, the world's nations spend some _____ *trillion* annually for military purposes.
    a) 5
    b) 4
    c) 1
    d) 8
    e) 2

23. *Military spending* accounts for _____ percent of the federal budget of the United States.
    a) less than 5
    b) 10
    c) 16
    d) 35
    e) 50

24. It is estimated that there are now _____ countries that possess nuclear weapons.
    a) 1
    b) 3
    c) 5
    d) 8
    e) 10

25. Which of the following was *not* listed as a means of reducing the danger of war?
    a) deterrence
    b) high-technology defence
    c) diplomacy and disarmament
    d) resolving underlying conflict
    e) multi-national corporate investment

26. Experts predict that by 2010 as many as _____ nations could have the ability to fight a nuclear war.
    a) 20
    b) 30
    c) 40
    d) 50

Matching: Economics

1. _____ The social institution that organizes a society's production, distribution, and consumption of goods and services.

2. _____ A production system based on service work and extensive use of information.

3. ____ The part of the economy that transforms raw materials into manufactured goods.
4. ____ The part of the economy involving services rather than goods.
5. ____ Economic activity spanning many nations of the world with little regard for national borders.
6. ____ An economic system in which natural resources and the means of producing goods and services are collectively owned.
7. ____ An economic and political system in which companies are privately owned although they cooperate closely with the government.
8. ____ An organized sphere of social life, or societal subsystem, designed to meet human needs.
9. ____ An organization with a legal existence, including rights and liabilities, apart from those of its members.
10. ____ Giant corporations composed of many smaller corporations.

a. socialism
b. conglomerates
c. secondary sector
d. tertiary sector
e. social institution
f. state capitalism
g. economy
h. post-industrial economy
i. global economy
j. corporation

Matching: Politics
1. ____ The ability to achieve desired ends despite resistance.
2. ____ Power people perceive as legitimate rather than coercive.
3. ____ A highly centralized political system that extensively regulates people's lives.
4. ____ A political system that denies popular participation in government.
5. ____ Tax revenues as a share of the gross domestic product for Canada in 1996.
6. ____ The percentage of eligible voters who voted in the 2000 federal election.
7. ____ An analysis of politics that views power as dispersed among many competing interest groups.
8. ____ An analysis of politics that views power as concentrated among the rich.
9. ____ Acts of violence or the threat of such violence by an individual or group as a political strategy.
10. ____ Organized, armed conflict among the people of various societies, directed by their government.

a. power-elite model
b. war
c. authoritarianism
d. authority
e. terrorism
f. 63
g. pluralist model
h. power
i. 43.4
j. totalitarianism

Fill-in-the-blank: Economics
1. A _____ _____ refers to an organized sphere of social life, or societal subsystem, designed to meet human needs.

Society: The Basics, Second Canadian Edition

2. _____ range from necessities like food to luxuries like swimming pools, while _____ include various activities that benefit others.

3. *Industrialization* introduced five fundamental changes in the economies of Western societies, including: new sources of _____, the centralization of work in _____, manufacturing and _____ _____, _____, and _____ _____.

4. A _____-_____ *economy* is a productive system based on service work and high technology.

5. The Information Revolution unleashed three key changes, including: From tangible products to _____, from mechanical skills to _____ skills, and the movement of work from factories to _____ _____.

6. The _____ _____ is the part of the economy generating raw materials directly from the natural environment.

7. The _____ _____ is the part of the economy generating services rather than goods.

8. Four major consequences of a *global economy* include: a global _____ _____, an increasing number of products passing through the _____ of more than one nation, _____ _____ no longer control the economic activity that takes place within their boundaries, and a _____ number of businesses, operating internationally, control a vast share of the world's economic activity.

9. A *capitalist system* has three distinctive features, including: _____ ownership of property, pursuit of personal _____, and _____ and consumer choice.

200

10. A *socialist system* has three distinctive features, including: _____ ownership of property, pursuit of _____ goals, and _____ control of the economy.

11. _____ _____ is an economic and political system in which companies are privately owned although they cooperate closely with the government.

12. A comparison of economic performance between *capitalist* and *socialist* economies supports the conclusion that capital economies produce a _____ overall standard of living but with _____ income disparity.

13. *Socialist* systems in Eastern Europe prior to the great transformations of 1989 and 1990 did away with _____ *elites*, but expanded the clout of _____ *elites*.

14. While _____ percent of males over the age of 16 in Canada have income-producing jobs, _____ of the females do.

15. The changing Canadian economy has, since 1980, seen a relatively constant membership in _____ _____, organizations that seek to improve wages and working conditions.

16. In the year 2000, _____ percent of *new jobs* were in the service sector, and _____ percent of the *labour force* performed service work.

17. People describe their occupations as *professions* to the extent that they demonstrate the following four characteristics: _____ knowledge, _____ practice, _____ over clients, and _____ to community rather than to self-interest.

18. The *Information Revolution* is changing the kind of work people do as well as where they do it. Computers are altering the character of work in four additional ways: they are _____ labour, making work more _____, _____ workplace interaction, and enhancing employer's _____ of workers.

Society: The Basics, Second Canadian Edition

19. _____ are giant corporations comprised of many smaller corporations.

20. _____ refers to domination of a market by a few producers.

Fill-in-the-blank: Politics

1. _____ is the social institution that distributes power, sets a social agenda, and makes decisions.

2. *Power* people perceive as legitimate rather than coercive is referred to as _____.

3. Max Weber differentiated between three types of *authority*, including _____, _____-_____, and _____.

4. _____ *authority* is power legitimated through extraordinary personal abilities that inspire devotion and obedience.

5. All European societies where royal families remain are _____ *monarchies*.

6. A _____ is a political system in which a single family rules from generation to generation.

7. According to the authors, countries like Canada are not truly *democratic* for two reasons. One, there is the problem of _____. The vast majority of political officials are not elected. Two, there is the problem of economic _____.

8. _____ is a political system that denies popular participation in government.

9. _____ refers to a political system that extensively regulates people's lives.

10. A _____ _____ refers to a range of government agencies and programs that provides benefits to the population.

Study Guide

11. The nineteenth-century poet and essayist Ralph Waldo Emerson said, "The government that governs best is the government that governs _____."

12. The Canadian *welfare state* is smaller than that in many industrial nations. As measured by *tax revenues as a share of gross domestic product*, Scandinavian countries like Denmark and Sweden have relative large welfare states (56.1 and 63,0 respectively). In Canada the comparable figure is _____ percent.

13. One major cluster of attitudes related to the *political spectrum* concerns _____ issues, while another concerns _____ issues.

14. In 2000, while the Liberal party enjoyed about 40 percent popular support, the NDP struggled at around _____ percent.

15. The _____-_____ *model*, closely allied with the *social-conflict paradigm*, is an analysis of politics that views power as concentrated among the rich.

16. The _____ _____-_____ *model* is an analysis that explains politics in terms of the operation of a society's economic system.

17. While conservatives suggest *voter apathy* amounts to an _____ to politics, liberals counter that most non-voters are _____ from politics.

18. Analysts claim *revolutions* share a number of traits, including: rising _____, _____ government, _____ leadership by intellectuals, and establishing a new _____.

19. According to Paul Johnson, *terrorism* has four distinguishing characteristics, including: terrorists try to paint violence as a _____ political tactic, terrorism is employed not just by groups, but also by _____ against their own people, democratic societies reject terrorism in principle, but they are especially _____ to terrorists because they afford extensive civil liberties to their people, and terrorism is always a matter of _____.

203

20. *Quincy Wright* cites five factors that promote *war*, including: perceived _____, social _____, _____ objectives, _____ imperatives, and the absence of _____.

Definition and Short-Answer: Economics

1. What were the five revolutionary changes brought about by the *Industrial Revolution*?
2. Define the concept *post-industrial society*, and identify three key changes unleashed by the *Information Revolution*.
3. What are the three basic characteristics of *capitalism*? What are the three basic characteristics of *socialism*? What is *democratic socialism*?
4. Comparing productivity and economic equality measures for *capitalist* and *socialist* economic systems, what are the relative advantages and disadvantages of each? Make comparisons in terms of *productivity, economic inequality,* and *civil liberties*.
5. What are three main consequences of the development of a *global economy*?
6. What are the three major *sectors* of the economy? Define and illustrate each of these.
7. What are the basic characteristics of a *profession*?
8. What are your interpretations of the data being presented in *Figure 12-2*?

Definition and Short-Answer: Politics

1. Differentiate between the concepts *power* and *authority*.
2. Differentiate between *Max Weber's* three types of *authority*.
3. Four types of *political systems* are reviewed in the text. Identify and describe each of these systems.
4. What are the general patterns in attitudes among Canadians concerning *social* and *economic issues* as reviewed in the text?
5. What is the evidence that *voter apathy* is a problem in our society? What are its causes?
6. Discuss the *changing work place* using demographic data presented in the text. What are three changes that you think are positive? What are three changes you think are negative?
7. Differentiate between the *pluralist* and *power-elite* models concerning the distribution of power in Canada.
8. What are the four general patterns identified in the text concerning *revolutions*?
9. What are the five factors identified in the text as promoting *war*?
10. Several approaches to reducing the chances for *nuclear war* are addressed in the text. Identify these approaches.
11. In what ways has politics gone global?
12. What are the four insights presented in the text concerning *terrorism*?

13. Discuss how the concepts of *democracy* and *freedom* are understood within the economic systems of *capitalism* and *socialism*.

PART VI: ANSWERS TO STUDY QUESTIONS

True-False: Economics
1. T (p. 278)
2. T (p. 278)
3. T (p. 279)
4. F (p. 279)
5. F (p. 279)
6. F (p. 279)
7. F (p. 282)
8. T (p. 283)
9. T (p. 283)
10. F (p. 283)
11. T (p. 284)
12. F (p. 284)
13. F (p. 286)
14. F (p. 286)
15. T (p. 287)
16. T (p. 288)
17. F (p. 288)
18. T (p. 288)

True-False: Politics
1. T (p. 291)
2. F (p. 291)
3. F (p. 291)
4. T (p. 292)
5. T (p. 293)
6. T (p. 294)
7. F (p. 295)
8. T (p. 295)
9. T (p. 295)
10. F (p. 296)
11. F (p. 297)
12. T (p. 297)
13. T (p. 297)
14. T (p. 298)
15. F (p. 298)
16. T (p. 300)
17. F (p. 301)
18. T (p. 302)
19. T (p. 302)
20. F (p. 302)

Multiple Choice: Economics
1. d (p. 278)
2. a (p. 279)
3. c (p. 279)
4. b (p. 279)
5. c (p. 279)
6. e (p. 279)
7. c (p. 279)
8. a (p. 280)
9. d (pp. 280-281)
10. d (p. 282)
11. d (p. 283)
12. e (p. 283)
13. b (p. 283)
14. a (p. 283)
15. b (p. 283)
16. e (p. 283)
17. e (p. 284)
18. e (p. 284)
19. c (p. 284)
20. b (p. 284)
21. a (p. 284)
22. c (p. 286)
23. e (p. 288)
24. e (pp. 287-288)
25. a (p. 288)
26. d (p. 288)
27. b (p. 288)
28. b (p. 288)
29. c (p. 288)
30. c (p. 291)

Multiple Choice Politics
1. b (p. 290)
2. e (p. 291)
3. d (p. 291)
4. a (p. 291)
5. c (p. 291)
6. c (pp. 291-292)
7. c (p. 292)
8. b (p. 292)
9. e (p. 295)
10. d (p. 295)
11. b (p. 295)
12. b (p. 295)
13. d (p. 297)
14. e (p. 297)
15. d (p. 298)
16. a (p. 298)
17. b (p. 298)
18. c (p. 299)
19. c (p. 300)
20. e (p. 300)
21. e (p. 301)
22. c (p. 301)
23. c (p. 302)
24. d (p. 302)
25. e (p. 302)
26. d (p. 302)

Matching: Economics
1. g (p. 278)
2. h (p. 279)
3. c (p. 279)
4. d (p. 279)
5. i (p. 279)
6. a (p. 282)
7. f (p. 283)
8. e (p. 278)
9. j (p. 288)
10. b (p. 288)

Matching: Politics
1. h (p. 290)
2. d (p. 291)
3. j (p. 292)
4. c (p. 292)
5. i (p. 295)
6. f (p. 297)
7. g (p. 298)
8. a (p. 298)
9. e (p. 300)
10. b (p. 301)

Fill-in-the-blank: Economics

1. social institution (p. 278)
2. goods, services (p. 278)
3. energy, factories, mass production, specialization, wage labour (p. 278)
4. post-industrial (p. 279)
5. ideas, literacy, almost anywhere (p. 279)
6. primary sector (p. 279)
7. tertiary sector (p. 279)
8. division of labour, economies, national governments, small (pp. 279-280)
9. private, profit, competition (p. 281)
10. collective, collective, government (p. 282)
11. State capitalism (p. 283)
12. higher, greater (p. 283)
13. economic, political (p. 284)
14. 66.8, 54.6 (p. 284)
15. labour unions (p. 284)
16. 90, 75 (p. 284)
17. theoretical, self-regulating, authority, orientation (p. 285)
18. deskilling, abstract, limiting, control (p. 288)
19. Conglomerates (p. 288)
20. Oligopoly (p. 288)

Fill-in-the-blank: Politics

1. Politics (p. 290)
2. authority (p. 291)
3. traditional, rational-legal, charismatic (p. 291)
4. charismatic (p. 291)
5. constitutional (p. 292)
6. monarchy (p. 291)
7. bureaucracy, inequality (p. 292)
8. authoritarianism (p. 292)
9. Totalitarianism (p. 292)
10. welfare state (p. 295)
11. least (p. 295)
12. 43.4 (p.295)
13. economic, social (p. 295)
14. 10 (p. 297)
15. power-elite (p. 298)
16. Marxist political-economy (p. 298)
17. indifference, alienated (p. 297)
18. expectations, unresponsive, radical, legitimacy (pp. 299-300)
19. legitimate, governments, vulnerable, definition (p. 300)
20. threats, problems, political, moral, alternatives (p. 301)

PART VII: IN FOCUS – IMPORTANT ISSUES

1. With examples from Canada, identify and describe the five fundamental ways in which *industrialization* changed the economy.

2. In what ways is *post-industrial society* different from industrial society?

3. What are the four major consequences of the *global economy*?
    A.

    B.

    C.

    D.

4. What are the three distinctive features of capitalism?
   A.

   B.

   C.

5. How is *justice* understood in a capitalist context?

6. What are the three distinctive features of *socialism*?
   A.

   B.

   C.

7. How is *justice* understood in a socialist context?

8. What are the relative advantages of capitalism and socialism in each of the following domains?
   A. economic productivity

   B. economic equality

C. personal freedom

9. Discuss the differences in how capitalists and socialists understand the concepts of *democracy* and *freedom*.

10. What are the differences concerning the major qualities of *industrial society* and *post-industrial society*?

11. What are the four characteristics of a *profession*?
    A.

    B.

    C.

    D.

12. The *unemployment rate* in Canada decreased in the late 1990s to around 7 percent and remained at that level for several years. What is *underemployment*? Why is it perhaps a bigger problem in our society than unemployment today?

13. What are the four ways in which *computers* are changing the character of work in Canada? Provide an illustration for each of these.

    Change   Illustration
    A.

    B.

    C.

    D.

14. Answer the following questions concerning corporations in Canada and their place within the global economy.
    A. What is the evidence that there is *economic concentration* in Canada?

    B. What are three important consequences of a *global economy*?

    C. What are three major patterns that are expected to continue to occur in terms of our economy?

15. How is *authority* different from *power*?

16. Define and illustrate *traditional* authority.

17. Define and illustrate *rational-legal* authority.

18. Define and illustrate *charismatic* authority.

19. How are each of the following categories of *political systems* defined? Provide an illustration for each.
    A. monarchy

    B. democracy

    C. authoritarianism

    D. totalitarianism

20. Describe the *political spectrum* in Canada. What strikes you most about the data presented in the text?

21. Generally discuss the evidence for *voter apathy* in Canada today. What are the two major explanations of voter apathy in Canada?

22. Differentiate between the following competing models of power in Canada. What is the evidence being used in support of each model?
    A. pluralist model

    B. power-elite model

    C. Marxist model

23. What are the four traits commonly shared by *revolutions?*

24. What are the four distinguishing characteristics of *terrorism?*

25. What are five factors that promote *war?* Illustrate each.

26. What are the four recent approaches to *peace* identified in the text? What are your thoughts on each in terms of promoting peace?

27. What are the three issues raised authors when they consider future political concerns? How would you solve them?

PART VIII: ANALYSIS AND COMMENT

Window on the World – Global Map 12-1
"Agricultural Employment in Global Perspective"

Key Points: Questions:

Window on the World – Global Map 12-2
"Service-Sector Employment in Global Perspective"

Key Points: Questions:

Society: The Basics, Second Canadian Edition

Seeing Ourselves – National Map 12-1
"Unemployment Rates Across Canada"
Key Points: Questions:

Social Diversity
"Diversity in the New Century: Changes in the Workplace"
Key Points: Questions:

Window on the World – Global Map 12-3
"Political Freedom in Global Perspective"
Key Points: Questions:

Critical Thinking
"Information Warfare: Let Your Fingers Do the Fighting"
Key Points: Questions:

Controversy and Debate
"Is Canada's Welfare State a 'Laggard'?"
Key Points: Questions:

Study Guide

Family and Religion

PART I: CHAPTER OUTLINE
1. The Family: Basic Concepts
2. The Family: Global Variations
    A. Marriage Patterns
    B. Residential Patterns
    C. Patterns of Descent
    D. Patterns of Authority
3. Theoretical Analysis of the Family
    A. Functions of the Family: Structural-Functional Analysis
    B. Inequality and the Family: Social-Conflict Analysis
    C. Constructing Family Life: Micro-Level Analysis
4. Stages of Family Life
    A. Courtship and Romantic Love
    B. Settling In: Ideal and Real Marriage
    C. Child Rearing
    D. The Family in Later Life
5. Canadian Families: Class, Race, and Gender
    A. Social Class
    B. Ethnicity and Race
    C. Gender
6. Transitions and Problems in Family Life
    A. Divorce
    B. Remarriage
    C. Family Violence
7. Alternative Family Forms
    A. One-Parent Families
    B. Cohabitation
    C. Gay and Lesbian Couples
    D. Singlehood
    E. New Reproductive Technology
    F. Looking Ahead: Family in the Twenty-First Century

215

8. Religion: Basic Concepts
9. Theoretical Analysis of Religion
    A. Functions of Religion: Structural-Functional Analysis
    B. Constructing the Sacred: Symbolic-Interaction Analysis
    C. Inequality and Religion: Social-Conflict Analysis
10. Religion and Social Change
    A. Max Weber: Protestantism and Capitalism
    B. Liberation Theology
11. Church, Sect, and Cult
12. Religion in History
13. Religion in Canada
    A. Religious Commitment
    B. Religion: Class, Gender, and Race
14. Religion in a Changing Society
    A. Secularization
    B. Civil Religion
    C. Religious Revival
    D. Looking Ahead: Religion in the Twenty-First Century
15. Summary
16. Key Concepts
17. Critical-Thinking Questions
18. Family
19. Applications and Exercises
20. Sites to See

PART II: LEARNING OBJECTIVES

1. To be able to define and illustrate basic concepts relating to the social institutions of kinship, family, and marriage.
2. To gain a cross-cultural perspectives of the social institutions of kinship, family, and marriage.
3. To be able to analyze the social institutions of kinship, family, and marriage using the structural-functional, social-conflict, and symbolic-interaction perspectives.
4. To be able to describe the traditional life course of the Canadian family.
5. To be able to recognize the impact of social class, race, ethnicity, and gender socialization on the family.
6. To be able describe the problems and transitions that seriously affect family life.
7. To be able to describe the composition and prevalence of alternative family forms.
8. To become aware of the impact, both technologically and ethically, of new reproductive techniques on the family.
9. To be able to identify five sociological conclusions about the family as we enter the twenty-first century.

10. To be able to define basic concepts relating to the sociological analysis of religion.
11. To be able to identify and describe the three functions of religion as developed by Emile Durkheim.
12. To be able to discuss the view that religion is socially constructed.
13. To be able to discuss the role of religion in maintaining social inequality.
14. To be able to describe how industrialization and science affect religious beliefs and practices.
15. To be able to compare and contrast the basic types of religious organization.
16. To be able to distinguish between pre-industrial and industrial societies in terms of religious beliefs and practices.
17. To be able to identify and generally distinguish between the world's major religions.
18. To be able to discuss the basic demographic patterns concerning religious affiliation, religiosity, secularization, and religious revival in Canada today.
19. To begin to critically think about the role of religion in the world as it will unfold over the next generation, and to consider the relationship between religion and science.

PART III: KEY CONCEPTS

Family:

cohabitation

descent

endogamy

exogamy

extended family

family

family unit

homogamy

kinship

marriage

monogamy

nuclear family

polygamy

Religion:

animism

charisma

church

civil religion

cult

denomination

faith

religious fundamentalism

liberation theology

profane

religion

religiosity

sacred

sect

secularization

state church

totem

PART IV: IMPORTANT RESEARCHERS

Family:

Jessie Bernard

Religion:

Emile Durkheim   Max Weber

Karl Marx

PART V: STUDY QUESTIONS

True-False: Family

1. T F When two gay couples married under the authority of an obscure section of the Ontario Marriage Act in 2001, the province immediately declared that the marriages would not be registered.
2. T F *Families of affinity* are comprised of people related by blood.
3. T F Because it is based on marriage, the nuclear family is also known as the *conjugal family*.
4. T F Norms of *endogamy* relate to marriage between people of the same social category.
5. T F *Matrilocality* occurs more commonly in societies that engage in distant warfare or in which daughters have greater economic value.
6. T F *Polyandry* is much more common around the world than is *polygyny*.
7. T F *Neolocality* refers to a residential pattern in which a married couple lives apart from the parents of both spouses.
8. T F Every known culture has some type of *incest taboo*.
9. T F Our society places less of an emphasis on *romantic love* than most other cultures around the world.
10. T F Economically speaking, industrialization transforms children from an asset to a *liability*.

11. T F While the actual number is smaller, the "ideal" number of children to have for most Canadians adults is three or more.
12. T F Most two-parent families with children under the age of 15 have one parent at home looking after children.
13. T F Parental leave in Canada is currently 12 months.
14. T F *Jessie Bernard's* research on marriage suggests that this institution is more beneficial for men than it is for women.
15. T F The *divorce rate* in Canada during the twentieth century has actually increased only slightly.
16. T F While the *divorce rate* in Canada is about the same as that in the U.S., it is much lower than that in Japan and Italy.
17. T F *Blended families* are composed of children and some combination of biological parents and stepparents.
18. T F According to the text, most *child abusers* are men.
19. T F Only rarely do cohabiting couples have children before they get married.
20. T F Cohabitation is most popular in Quebec.
21. T F *Homosexual marriages* are not officially registered in any Canadian province or territory.
22. T F The percentage of households with *single adults* has actually been decreasing over the last two decades.
23. T F *Test-tube babies* are, technically speaking, the result of the process of *in vitro fertilization*.
24. T F Our authors conclude that family life in the twenty-first century will be *highly variable*.

True-False: Religion

1. T F According to Emile Durkheim, the *profane* refers to that which is an ordinary element of everyday life.
2. T F Emile Durkheim defined a *totem* as an object in the natural world collectively defined as sacred.
3. T F According to Emile Durkheim, society has an existence and power of its own, beyond the lives of the people who collectively created it.
4. T F A major criticism of Emile Durkheim's analysis of religion is that he focuses too much attention on the *dysfunctions* of religious belief and practice.
5. T F The symbolic-interaction approach views religion as a *social construction*.
6. T F Social-conflict theory focuses on how religion promotes change and equality.
7. T F *Liberation theology* is a fusion of Christian Principles with political activism, often Marxist in character.
8. T F Two types, or forms, of churches identified in the text are the *church formally aligned with the state* and the *denomination*.

9. T F Whereas a *sect* is a type of religious organization that stands apart from the larger society, a *cult* represents something almost entirely new and stands outside a society's cultural tradition.

10. T F *Animism* is the belief that natural objects are conscious life forms that affect humanity.

11. T F Fewer than forty percent of people in the United States identify with a religion.

12. T F *Religiosity* refers to the importance of religion in a person's life.

13. T F By global standards, *North Americans* are relatively nonreligious people.

14. T F A quasi-religious loyalty based in citizenship is called a *civil religion*.

15. T F Fundamentalists reject religious pluralism.

16. T F Science and new technologies are reducing the relevance of religion in modern society as many moral dilemmas and spiritual issues are resolved or are diminishing in significance.

Multiple Choice: Family

1. Which of the following is *incorrect*?
   a) The marriage rate remained unchanged over the last 15 years.
   b) Divorces have increased 30 percent in the past 25 years.
   c) Almost 10 percent of marriages are predicted to end in divorce.
   d) Almost a third of children born today will live with a single parent at some time before reaching age 18.
   e) All of the above are incorrect.

2. Which of the following refers to a social bond, based on blood, marriage or adoption, that joins individuals into families?
   a) descent group
   b) nuclear family
   c) family
   d) kinship

3. The *consanguine family* is also known as the
   a) conjugal family.
   b) family of orientation.
   c) nuclear family.
   d) family of procreation.
   e) extended family.

4. What is the family unit including parents and children, as well as other kin?
   a) a family
   b) a kinship group
   c) a nuclear family
   d) an extended family

5. Which of the following cultural norms promotes the pattern of marriage between people of the *same social category*?
   a) endogamy
   b) monogamy
   c) exogamy
   d) polygamy

6. Marriage between people of different social categories is called
   a) polygamy.
   b) monogamy.
   c) exogamy.
   d) endogamy.

7. What is a marriage that joins *one female* with *more than one male*?
   a) polygamy
   b) polyandry
   c) endogamy
   d) polygyny

8. What is the residential pattern in which a married couple lives apart from the parents of both spouses?
   a) neolocality
   b) patrilocality
   c) matrilocality
   d) avunculocality
   e) bilateral descent

9. What is the system by which members of a society trace kinship over generations?
   a) family
   b) marriage
   c) descent
   d) extended family

10. Industrial societies, with greater gender equality, recognize _____ descent.
    a) cognilineal
    b) agnalineal
    c) bilateral
    d) neolateral

11. The type of sociological analysis of the family that holds that the family serves to perpetuate social inequality is
    a) social-exchange analysis.
    b) structural-functional analysis.
    c) social-conflict analysis.
    d) symbolic-interaction analysis.

12. Which theory and theorist traced the origin of the family to the need for men to pass property on to their sons?
    a) symbolic-interaction–George Herbert Mead
    b) structural-functionalism–Talcott Parsons
    c) structural-functionalism–Emile Durkheim
    d) social-conflict–Friedrich Engels

13. Which of the following is *not* one of the ways that families aid in the perpetuation of social inequality?
    a) property and inheritance
    b) bilateral descent
    c) patriarchy
    d) race and ethnicity

14. The depiction of courtship and marriage as forms of negotiation is found in the _____ *analysis*.
    a) structural-functional
    b) social-conflict
    c) symbolic-interaction
    d) social-exchange

15. Sociologists have noted that *romantic love* as a basis for marriage
    a) is reinforced by cultural values.
    b) acts as a strong incentive to leave one's original family of orientation to form a new family of procreation.
    c) is not as stable a basis for marriage as social and economic bases.
    d) all of the above

16. Most adults in Canada feel the *ideal number* of children is
    a) 1.
    b) 2.
    c) 3.
    d) 4.

17. Which of the following is *not* one of the familial adjustments made by parents in *later life*?
    a) adjustment to retirement and spending more time together
    b) helping to care for grandchildren
    c) assumption of more household responsibilities
    d) death of a spouse

18. The "sandwich generation" refers to
    a) the oldest baby boomers who simultaneously care for their own children and parents
    b) children who return to an empty home after school each day
    c) those raised on the white bread popular in the sixties
    d) those who have short mid-life career changes

19. Lillian Rubin focussed her research on the relationship between _____ and marriage.
    a) social class
    b) race
    c) presence of children
    d) age at marriage

20. Which group of women has the proportionately highest number of *lone parents*?
    a) Aboriginals
    b) Visible minorities
    c) Irish
    d) Swedish

21. Which of the following is *not* a finding of Jessie Bernard's study of marriage?
    a) married women have poorer mental health
    b) married women have more passive attitudes toward life
    c) married women report less personal happiness
    d) married women are not generally required to participate in the labour force

22. The high Canadian *divorce rate* has many causes; which of the following is *not* identified in the text as being one of them?
    a) Individualism is on the rise.
    b) Women are more dependent on men.
    c) Many marriages today are stressful.
    d) Romantic love often subsides.
    e) Divorce is easier to get and more socially acceptable.

23. Remarriage often creates families composed of both biological parents and stepparents and children. These are called
    a) second families.
    b) blended families.
    c) focal families.
    d) families of orientation.

24. In Canada, fathers were the perpetrators in _____ percent of sexual assaults against children.
    a) 8
    b) 38
    c) 68
    d) 98

25. Currently in Canada what percentage of families are one-parent families?
    a) 16
    b) 45
    c) 9
    d) 14

26. Which country, in 1989, became the first nation to legalize *same-sex marriages*?
    a) Denmark
    b) France
    c) the United States
    d) Japan

27. Which of the following statements is *not accurate* concerning *cohabitation*?
    a) It is more popular today in Canada than it was in 1980.
    b) One couple out of seven is a common-law relationship.
    c) Ontario has the highest rate of cohabitation.
    d) About half of cohabiting couples have at least one child living with them.
    e) Common-law unions have a higher rate of dissolution than do marriages.

28. Which of the following countries is the most accepting of childbirth outside of marriage?
   a) United States
   b) Canada
   c) Great Britain
   d) Spain
   e) Iceland

Multiple Choice: Religion

1. _____ is a term that refers to that which people set apart as extraordinary, inspiring a sense of awe and reverence.
   a) Profane
   b) Sacred
   c) Animism
   d) Religiosity

2. What is the term for the social institution involving beliefs and practices based upon a conception of the sacred?
   a) faith
   b) totem
   c) religion
   d) ritual

3. Emile Durkheim referred to the ordinary elements of everyday life as
   a) religion.
   b) faith.
   c) ritual.
   d) the profane.

4. Formal, ceremonial behaviour refers to
   a) the sacred.
   b) ritual.
   c) religion.
   d) faith.

5. Which of the following is a function of religion according to *Emile Durkheim*?
   a) social cohesion
   b) social control
   c) providing meaning and purpose
   d) all are functions identified by Emile Durkheim
   e) none are, as he saw religion as having negative consequences for society

6. The view that religion is completely *socially constructed* by a society's members is espoused by
   a) Max Weber.
   b) Peter Berger.
   c) Karl Marx.
   d) Emile Durkheim.

7. Which of the following is an appropriate criticism of a *symbolic-interactionist* approach to religion?
   a) It ignores religion's link to inequality.
   b) It fails to consider the importance of rituals.
   c) It treats reality as objective.
   d) It ignores the social construction of religion.
8. Who would be most likely to argue that religion motivates *capitalism*?
   a) a Marxist
   b) a symbolic interactionist
   c) a follower of Max Weber
   d) a person following the precepts of liberation theology
9. *Liberation theology* advocates a blending of religion with
   a) the family.
   b) the economy.
   c) education.
   d) politics.
10. A church, independent of the state, that accepts religious pluralism is a
    a) denomination.
    b) sect.
    c) cult.
    d) civil religion.
11. Which of the following is *not* a feature of a *sect*?
    a) charismatic leaders
    b) psychic intensity and informal structure
    c) membership through conversion
    d) proselytizing
    e) all of the above are features of a sect
12. A religious organization that is largely outside society's cultural traditions is called a
    a) totem.
    b) cult.
    c) ecclesia.
    d) sect.
13. The belief that elements of the natural world are conscious life forms that affect humanity refers to
    a) animism.
    b) cults.
    c) a totem.
    d) sects.
14. Approximately ____ percent of people in Canada identify with a religion.
    a) 26
    b) 49
    c) 68
    d) 80
    e) 98

15. The importance of religion in a person's life is called
    a) ideology.
    b) ritual.
    c) religiosity.
    d) affiliation.

16. What is *secularization*?
    a) the ecumenical movement
    b) the historical decline in the importance of the supernatural and the sacred
    c) the increase in religiosity in post-industrial society
    d) fundamentalism

17. A quasi-religious loyalty binding individuals in a basically secular society is referred to as
    a) a totem.
    b) secularization.
    c) religiosity.
    d) fundamentalism.
    e) civil religion.

18. Which of the following is *not* identified in the text as a distinction of *religious fundamentalism*?
    a) Fundamentalists interpret sacred texts literally.
    b) Fundamentalists promote religious pluralism.
    c) Fundamentalists pursue the personal experience of God's presence.
    d) Fundamentalism opposes "secular humanism."
    e) Many fundamentalists endorse conservative political goals.

Matching: Family

1. _____ A family unit including parents, children, as well as other kin.
2. _____ People with or without legal or blood ties who feel they belong together and want to define themselves as a family.
3. _____ The system by which members of a society trace kinship over generations.
4. _____ Marriage between people of the same social category.
5. _____ A residential pattern in which a married couple lives apart from the parents of both spouses.
6. _____ A form of marriage uniting one female with more than one male.
7. _____ A system tracing kinship through both men and women.
8. _____ A form of marriage uniting one male with more than one female.
9. _____ The feeling of affection and sexual passion toward another person as the basis of marriage.
10. _____ Families composed of children and some combination of biological parents and stepparents.

a. endogamy
b. extended family
c. blended families
d. bilateral decent
e. descent
f. neolocality
g. family of affinity
h. polygyny
i. polyandry
j. romantic love

Matching: Religion

1. ____ That which is an ordinary element of everyday life.
2. ____ The social institution involving beliefs and practices based upon a conception of the sacred.
3. ____ Belief anchored in conviction rather than scientific evidence.
4. ____ An object in the natural world collectively defined as sacred.
5. ____ Suggested that the religious doctrine of Calvinism sparked the Industrial Revolution in Western Europe.
6. ____ A type of religious organization well integrated into the larger society.
7. ____ A church, independent of the state, that accepts religious pluralism.
8. ____ Extraordinary personal qualities that can turn an audience into followers.
9. ____ A type of religious organization that stands apart from the larger society.
10. ____ A religious organization that is largely outside a society's cultural traditions.
11. ____ A fusion of Christian principles with political activism, often Marxist in character.
12. ____ The importance of religion in a person's life.
13. ____ The historical decline in the importance of the supernatural and the sacred.
14. ____ A conservative religious doctrine that opposes intellectualism and worldly accommodation in favour of restoring traditional, otherworldly spirituality.

a. denomination
b. fundamentalism
c. religiosity
d. religion
e. charisma
f. profane
g. liberation theology
h. sacred
i. church
j. faith
k. totem
l. secularization
m. cult
n. Max Weber
o. Emile Durkheim
p. sect

Fill-in-the-blank: Family

1. The _____ is a social institution found in all societies that unites individuals into cooperative groups that oversee the bearing and raising of children.

2. _____ refers to a social bond, based on blood, marriage, or adoption, that joins individuals into families.

3. The _____ *family* is based on blood ties.

4. _____ refers to marriage between people of the same social group or category.

5. _____ is a marriage that joins one female with more than one male.

6. _____ refers to the system by which members of a society trace kinship over generations.

7. _____ *descent* is a system tracing kinship through both men and women.
8. The predominance of *polygyny, patrilocality,* and *patrilineal descent* reflects the global pattern of _____.
9. Structural-functionalists identify several *vital tasks* performed by the family. These include: _____, _____ of sexual activity, social _____, and material and economic _____.
10. Cultural norms that forbid sexual relationships or marriage between specified kin are called _____ _____.
11. *Social-conflict* theorists argue that families perpetuate social inequality in several ways, including: Property and _____, _____, and _____ and _____.
12. Our culture celebrates _____ _____–the feeling of affection and sexual passion toward another person–as the basis for marriage.
13. _____ *percent* of Canadians identify raising children as integral to personal fulfilment.
14. _____ percent of all Aboriginal women aged 15-64 are lone parents.
15. Jessie Bernard suggests that every marriage is actually _____ different relationships.
16. The high Canadian *divorce rate* has many causes, including: _____ is on the rise, _____ _____ often subsides, women are now less _____ on men, many of today's marriages are _____, divorce is more socially _____, and from a legal standpoint, divorce is _____ to obtain.
17. After separation, mothers gain *custody* over children in over _____ of the cases.
18. Remarriage often creates _____ *families*, composed of children and some combination of biological parents and stepparents.
19. Estimates suggest that _____ Canadian women have been victims of spousal violence in the last five years.

20. While women are only slightly more likely to be victims of spousal abuse than are men, women are much more likely to be severely abused by their partner. Women are also more likely to be victims of _____ spousal violence.

21. *Family violence* includes _____, _____, or _____ abuse of one family member by another.

22. _____ is the sharing of a household by an unmarried couple.

23. *Test-tube babies* are the result of _____ _____ _____.

24. Sociologists point out five probable *future trends* regarding the family. These include: _____ rates are likely to remain high, family life will be more _____ than ever, men are likely to continue to play a limited role in _____ _____, we will continue to feel the effects of _____ change in our families, and the importance of new _____ technology will increase.

Fill-in-the-blank: Religion

1. *Emile Durkheim* labelled the ordinary elements of everyday life the _____.

2. A _____ is a natural object—or its representation—collectively defined as sacred.

3. _____ refers to belief anchored in conviction rather than scientific evidence.

4. According to Emile Durkheim, three major *functions of religion* include: Social _____, social _____, and providing _____ and _____.

5. According to *Max Weber*, industrial capitalism developed in the wake of _____.

6. _____ *theology* is a fusion of Christian principles with political activism, often Marxist in character.

7. A _____ is a type of religious organization well integrated into the larger society.

8. _____ refers to extraordinary personal qualities that can turn audiences into followers.

9. _____ is the belief that natural objects are conscious forms of life that can affect humanity.

10. _____ refers to the importance of religion in a person's life.

11. By far, the largest proportion of Canadians declare themselves to be _____ _____ when asked about religious identification.

12. The historical decline in the importance of the supernatural and the sacred is referred to as _____.

13. A _____ religion is a quasi-religious loyalty based on citizenship.

14. *Religious fundamentalism* is distinctive in five ways, including: interpreting sacred texts _____, rejecting religious _____, pursuing the personal experience of God's _____, opposition to secular _____, and endorsement of _____ political goals.

Definition and Short-Answer: Family

1. What are the four basic *functions* of the family according to structural-functionalists?
2. Define and describe the three patterns of *descent*.
3. Why has the *divorce rate* increased in recent decades in Canada? What are the basic demographic patterns involving divorce in our society today?
4. What are the four *stages* of the family life cycle outlined in the text? Describe the major events occurring during each of these stages.
5. In what ways are *middle-class* and *working-class* marriages different?
6. What are the arguments being made about the family by *social-conflict* theorists?
7. How has the role of children in the family changed over time?
8. What are the dimensions of *family violence*? What are the demographic patterns concerning each of these?
9. Five *alternative family forms* are discussed in the text. Identify these and review the data concerning three of them. What are your opinions concerning these changes in the family?
10. What are the five conclusions being made about marriage and family life into the twenty-first century?

Definition and Short-Answer: Religion

1. According to *structural-functional* analysis, what are three major functions of religion? Provide an example for each from Canadian society.
2. Discuss *Max Weber's* points concerning the historical relationship between Protestantism and capitalism.

3. How do theorists operating from the *social conflict* perspective understand religion and how it operates in society? Provide two examples to illustrate.
4. In a one-page written discussion, debate the issue of whether science threatens or strengthens religion in society.
5. Discuss the issue concerning the extent of *religiosity* in Canada today.
6. Briefly describe the position of religious *fundamentalism* in our society today.
7. Discuss the relationship between *religion* and *social stratification* in Canada.
8. Differentiate between the nature of religion in *pre-industrial* and *industrial* societies.
9. Differentiate between *civil religion* and *religious fundamentalism*.
10. Discuss the relationship between religion and science.

PART V: ANSWERS TO STUDY QUESTIONS

True-False: Family
1. T (pp.309-310)
2. F (p. 310)
3. T (p. 311)
4. T (p. 337)
5. T (p. 311)
6. F (p. 311)
7. T (pp.311-311)
8. T (p. 313)
9. F (p. 315)
10. T (p. 316)
11. F (p. 317)
12. F (p. 317)
13. T (p. 317)
14. T (p. 319)
15. F (p. 320)
16. F (p. 320)
17. T (p. 321)
18. T (p. 323)
19. F (p. 324)
20. T (p. 324)
21. T (p. 324)
22. F (p. 324)
23. T (p. 325)
24. T (p. 325)

True-False: Religion
1. T (p. 326)
2. T (p. 327)
3. T (p. 327)
4. F (p. 327)
5. T (p. 328)
6. F (p. 329)
7. T (p. 331)
8. T (p. 332)
9. T (p. 332)
10. T (p. 333)
11. F (p. 333)
12. T (p. 333)
13. F (p. 333)
14. T (p. 335)
15. T (p. 336)
16. F (p. 339)

Multiple Choice: Family
1. e (p. 310)
2. d (p. 310)
3. e (p. 310)
4. d (p. 310)
5. a (p. 311)
6. c (p. 311)
7. b (p. 311)
8. a (pp.311-312)
9. c (p. 312)
10. c (p. 312)
11. c (p. 313)
12. d (p. 313)
13. b (p. 313)
14. d (p. 314)
15. d (pp.315-316)
16. b (p. 317)
17. c (pp.317-318)
18. a (p. 318)
19. a (p. 318)
20. a (p. 319)
21. d (p. 319)
22. b (p. 320)
23. b (p. 321)
24. d (p. 323)
25. d (p. 323)
26. a (p. 324)
27. c (p. 324)
28. e (p. 325)

Multiple Choice: Religion
1. b (p. 326)
2. c (p. 326)
3. d (p. 326)
4. b (p. 326)
5. d (p. 527)
6. b (p. 328)
7. a (p. 328)
8. a (p. 329)
9. d (p. 331)
10. a (p. 332)
11. e (p. 332)
12. b (p. 332)
13. a (p. 333)
14. d (p. 333)
15. c (p. 333)
16. b (p. 335)
17. e (p. 335)
18. b (p. 336)

Matching: Family
1. b (p. 310)
2. g (p. 310)
3. e (p. 312)
4. a (p. 311)
5. f (pp.311-312)
6. i (p. 311)
7. d (p. 312)
8. h (p. 311)
9. j (p. 315)
10. c (p. 321)

Matching: Religion
1. f (p. 326)
2. d (p. 326)
3. j (p. 327)
4. k (p. 327)
5. n (p. 330)
6. i (p. 331)
7. a (p. 332)
8. e (p. 332)
9. p (p. 332)
10. m (p. 332)
11. g (p. 331)
12. c (p. 333)
13. l (p. 335)
14. b (p. 336)

Fill-in-the-blank: Family
1. family (p. 310)
2. Kinship (p. 310)
3. consanguine (p. 310)
4. Endogamy (p. 311)
5. Polyandry (p. 311)
6. Descent (p. 312)
7. Bilateral (p. 312)
8. patriarchy (p. 313)
9. socialization, regulation, placement, security (p. 313)
10. incest taboos (p. 313)
11. inheritance, patriarchy, race, ethnicity (p. 313)
12. romantic love (p. 315)
13. 60 (p. 316)
14. 18 (p. 319)
15. two (p. 319)
16. individualism, romantic love, dependent, stressful, acceptable, easier (p. 320)
17. 80 (p. 320)
18. blended (p. 321)
19. 700 000 (p. 321)
20. repeat (p. 321)
21. emotional, physical, sexual (p. 321)
22. Cohabitation (p. 324)
23. in vitro fertilization (p. 325)
24. divorce, diverse, child rearing, economic, reproductive (pp. 325-320)

Fill-in-the-blank: Religion
1. profane (p. 326)
2. totem (p. 327)
3. Faith (p. 327)
4. cohesion, control, meaning, purpose (p. 327)
5. Calvinism (p. 330)
6. Liberation (p. 331)
7. church (p. 331)
8. Charisma (p. 332)
9. Animism (p. 333)
10. Religiosity (p. 333)
11. Roman Catholic (p. 334)
12. secularization (p. 335)
13. civil (p. 335)
14. literally, pluralism, presence, humanism, conservative (pp. 336-337)

Society: The Basics, Second Canadian Edition

PART VII: IN FOCUS – IMPORTANT ISSUES

1. Define each of the following concepts.
   A. Family

   B. Family Unit

   C. Kinship

   D. Marriage

2. Identify and define or illustrate the different *patterns* found around the world for each of the following.
   A. Marriage

   B. Residence

   C. Descent

   D. Authority

3. According to structural-functionalists, what are the *functions* performed by families? Provide one piece of evidence for each function.

4. In what ways do *conflict theorists* believe the family perpetuates inequality? Illustrate or define each of these.

5. Micro-level approaches explore how individuals shape and experience family life. Differentiate between the following two micro-level perspectives.
    A. Symbolic-Interaction Analysis

    B. Social-Exchange Analysis

6. Briefly describe the content for each of the following stages in family life.
    A. Courtship

B. Settling In

C. Child Rearing

D. The Family in Later Life

7. Summarize the findings concerning Lillian Rubin's research on the relationship between *social class* and the family.

8. As they relate to the family, identify important demographic differences between Aboriginals, visible minorities and other Canadians.

9. Summarize the conclusions of Jessie Bernard concerning *gender* and the family.

10. What are the major causes of *divorce* as listed in the text? Illustrate each of these.

11. What are the characteristics most associated with divorce?

12. How common is *remarriage*?

13. Identify three important facts concerning each of the following two types of *family violence*.
    A. Violence against women

    B. Violence against children

14. Identify two important demographic facts concerning *single-parent families* in our society today.

15. How common is *cohabitation* in our society today?

16. What are two important points being made about *gay and lesbian couples*?

17. How common is *singlehood* in our society today?

18. What is *in vitro fertilization*?

19. What are the five likely trends for the family of the twenty-first century as identified by the authors?

20. How do sociologists conceptualize and understand the place of *faith* and *ritual* in the institution of religion?

21. Provide an illustration for Emile Durkheim's distinction between the *profane* and the *sacred*.

22. According to *structural-functionalist* Emile Durkheim, what are the three basic *functions of religion*? Provide an illustration for each of these.

23. What points are being made by *symbolic-interactionist* Peter Berger concerning religion?

24. How did *conflict theorist* Karl Marx understand religion?

25. What is Max Weber's point concerning the relationship between *Protestantism* and *capitalism*?

26. Differentiate between each of the following.
    A. Church

    B. Sect

    C. Cult

27. How is religion different in *pre-industrial societies* as compared with industrial societies? What are the similarities?

28. How religious are we here in Canada? What is the evidence?

29. What is the relationship between *social stratification* and religion?

30. Briefly discuss the place of each of the following patterns in Canada today.
    A. Secularism

    B. Civil Religion

    C. Religious Revival

31. What conclusions are being made by the authors concerning the place of religion in contemporary society?

PART VIII: ANALYSIS AND COMMENT

Window on the World – Global Map 13-1
"Marital Form in Global Perspective"
Key Points: Questions:

Society: The Basics, Second Canadian Edition

Global Sociology
"Early To Wed: A Report From Rural India"
Key Points: Questions:

Seeing Ourselves – National Map 13-1
"Single-Parent Families across Canada"
Key Points: Questions:

Controversy and Debate
"Should We Save the Traditional Family?"
Key Points: Questions:

Controversy and Debate
"Does Science Threaten Religion?"
Key Points: Questions:

Study Guide

14

Education and Health

PART I: CHAPTER OUTLINE

1. Education: A Global Survey
   A. Schooling in Low-Income Countries
   B. Schooling in High-Income Countries
   C. Schooling in Canada
2. The Functions of Schooling
3. Schooling and Social Inequality
   A. Public and Private Schools
   B. Access to Higher Education
   C. Credentialism
   D. Privilege and Personal Merit
4. Problems in the Schools
   A. Discipline and Violence
   B. Bureaucracy and Student Passivity
   C. The Academy: The Silent Classroom
   D. Dropping Out
   E. Academic Standards
   F. Looking Ahead: Schooling in the Twenty-First Century
5. Health
   A. Health and Society
6. Health: A Global Survey
   A. Health in Low-Income Countries
   B. Health in High-Income Countries
7. Health in Canada
   A. Who Is Healthy? Age, Gender, Class, and Race
   B. Cigarette Smoking
   C. Eating Disorders
   D. Sexually Transmitted Diseases
   E. Ethical Issues Surrounding Death
8. The Medical Establishment
   A. The Rise of Scientific Medicine
   B. Holistic Health
   C. Paying for Health: A Global Survey
   D. The Canadian Health Care System

9. Theoretical Analysis of Medicine
   A. Structural-Functional Analysis
   B. Symbolic-Interaction Analysis
   C. Social Conflict Analysis
   D. Looking Ahead: Health in the Twenty-First Century
10. Summary
11. Key Concepts
12. Critical-Thinking Questions
13. Exercises and Applications
14. Sites to See

PART II: LEARNING OBJECTIVES

1. To be able to describe the different role of education in low-income and high-income countries.
2. To compare education in India, the United States, and Japan to that provided in Canada.
3. To be able to identify and describe the functions of schooling.
4. To consider how education supports social inequality.
5. To be able to discuss the major issues and problems facing contemporary education in Canada today.
6. To be able to identify and evaluate alternatives to the current structure of the institution of education in our society.
7. To become aware of the ways in which the health of a population is shaped by society.
8. To develop a global and historical perspective on health and illness.
9. To recognize how age, gender, social class, ethnicity and race affect the health of individuals in our society.
10. To be able to discuss cigarette smoking, eating disorders, and sexually transmitted diseases as serious health problems in our society.
11. To be able to recognize and evaluate ethical issues surrounding dying and death.
12. To be able to compare and evaluate the relative effectiveness of scientific medicine and holistic medicine.
13. To be able to compare and evaluate the relative effectiveness of medicine in socialist and capitalist societies.
14. To be able to differentiate between the viewpoints being provided by the three major sociological perspectives concerning the medical establishment and health care.

PART IV: KEY CONCEPTS

Education:
credentialism

education

functional illiteracy

streaming or tracking

schooling

Medicine:

direct-fee system

euthanasia

health

holistic health

medicine

sick role

social epidemiology

socialized health care

PART IV: IMPORTANT RESEARCHERS

Education:

David Karp and William Yoels

Egerton Ryerson

James Coleman

Samuel Bowles and Herbert Gintis

Theodore Sizer

Randall Collins

Society: The Basics, Second Canadian Edition

Health:

Talcott Parsons   Joan Emerson

Erving Goffman

PART V: STUDY QUESTIONS

True-False: Education

1. T F Canada actually has a *higher* illiteracy rate than most Latin American societies.
2. T F Today, schooling in *low-income nations* is very homogenous because it reflects the global culture.
3. T F Japan still does not have national *mandatory education laws*.
4. T F Canada graduates a *smaller percentage* of its students from high school than does Japan.
5. T F The United States was among the first nations to endorse the principle of *mass education*.
6. T F Canada has a *smaller* percentage of those aged 25 to 64 holding a university or college degree than most other industrialized societies.
7. T F About 39 percent of those aged 25 to 64 in Canada have a *university or college degree*.
8. T F Teachers have always been valued in Canadian society. They earned many times the wages of a day labourer 100 years ago.
9. T F Social diversification is an important function of schooling according to structural-functional analysis.
10. T F A latent function of schooling is that it provides child care.
11. T F *Social conflict* theorists support *tracking* in that they believe it gives students the kind of learning that fits their abilities and motivation.
12. T F Roughly 5 percent of elementary and secondary school children in Canada attend *public schools*.
13. T F Of those aged 20 to 29, more females than males have attained post-secondary diplomas or degrees.

14. T F The amount graduates owed on student loans two years after graduation actually decreased between 1988 and 1997.
15. T F There is often little relationship between the credentials required for, and the responsibilities of, a specific job.
16. T F About 5 percent of those who leave a post-secondary school have not finished their program requirement.
17. T F Canadian students spend fewer days in school than students in many other high-income nations.
18. T F In 1998 there were more females than males enrolled in Canadian medical schools.

True-False: Health
1. T F The World Health Organization defines *health* as simply the absence of disease.
2. T F The top five causes of death in Canada have changed very little since 1900.
3. T F Sex is a stronger predictor of health than race.
4. T F Generally speaking, the less schooling people have the greater their chances of *smoking*.
5. T F An *eating disorder* is defined as an intense form of dieting or other unhealthy method of weight control.
6. T F Genital herpes can be deadly to newborns.
7. T F Almost seventy percent of all global *HIV cases* are recorded in sub-Saharan Africa.
8. T F HIV is both *infectious* and *contagious*.
9. T F Prevention is currently the most effective weapon against AIDS.
10. T F Medical and legal experts define *death* as the ceasing of any signs of cardiovascular and respiratory functioning.
11. T F It is illegal in Canada to assist in a suicide.
12. T F The first Medical Act came into force in 1935.
13. T F *Holistic medicine* stresses that physicians have to take the primary responsibility for health care in society.
14. T F About 16 percent of people in the United States have no health insurance at all.
15. T F The U.S. is unique among industrialized societies in lacking government programs that ensure basic medical care to every citizen.
16. T F Most physicians in Canada are salaried workers.
17. T F Most Canadians think that education is a much more important social issue than health care.
18. T F One criticism of the *symbolic-interaction* paradigm is that this approach seems to deny that there are any objective standards of well-being.
19. T F According to the *conflict approach* social inequality is the reasons some people have better health than others.

Society: The Basics, Second Canadian Edition

20. T F The most common objection to the *conflict approach* is that it minimizes the gains in Canadian health brought about by scientific medicine and higher living standards.

Multiple Choice: Education

1. The social institution guiding a society's transmission of knowledge—including basic facts, job skills, and also cultural norms and values—to its members is the definition for
   a) education.
   b) schooling.
   c) teaching.
   d) curriculum.

2. Half the population in the United States between the ages of 5 and 19 were enrolled in school by_____.
   a) 1650
   b) 1750
   c) 1850
   d) 1950

3. Formal instruction under the direction of specially trained teachers refers to
   a) curriculum.
   b) education.
   c) schooling.
   d) mainstreaming.

4. Which of the following is *inaccurate* concerning India?
   a) People earn about five percent of the income standard in Canada, and poor families often depend on the earnings of children.
   b) Less than one-half of Indian children enter secondary school.
   c) About one-half of the Indian population is illiterate.
   d) More girls than boys in India reach secondary school.

5. *Mandatory education* laws were found in every state in the United States by
   a) 1781.
   b) 1850.
   c) 1822.
   d) 1918.

6. Which of the following is/are accurate concerning education and schooling in Japan?
   a) Industrialization brought mandatory education to Japan in 1872.
   b) The Japanese system is praised for producing some of the world's highest achievers.
   c) About half of all Japanese students attend cram schools to prepare for exams.
   d) More men and women graduate from high school in Japan than in Canada.
   e) All of the above are accurate.

7. Which of the following nations has the highest percentage of adults with a *university or college degree*?
   a) Canada
   b) the United States
   c) Japan
   d) India

8. According to *structural-functionalists*, which of the following functions of formal education helps forge a population into a single, unified society?
   a) socialization
   b) social placement
   c) social integration
   d) cultural innovation

9. Which of the following is *not* identified by conflict theorists as a part of schooling that causes and perpetuates inequality?
   a) social control
   b) subsidized tuition
   c) testing
   d) tracking

10. Child care, establishing relationships and networks, and consuming the time and energy of teenagers are examples of
    a) the latent functions of education.
    b) school tracking.
    c) social control.
    d) mainstreaming.

11. *Structural-functionalists* overlook one core truth:
    a) education serves as a form of social placement.
    b) schooling helps to reproduce the class structure in each generation.
    c) schools serve several latent functions.
    d) schooling helps forge a mass of people into a unified society.
    e) education creates as well as transmits culture.

12. *Social-conflict* analysis associates formal education with
    a) student's skill enhancement.
    b) the improvement of personal well-being.
    c) patterns of social inequality.
    d) global competitiveness.

13. *Social conflict analysis* uses the term _____ to refer to the assignment of students to different types of educational programs.
    a) hierarchical education
    b) residual education
    c) ability placement
    d) competitive placement
    e) tracking

Society: The Basics, Second Canadian Edition

14. Most Canadians
    a) would send their child to a private school with an annual tuition fee of $5000.
    b) attend private school at some point during their elementary and secondary enrollment.
    c) show a growing satisfaction with the public school system.
    d) think that students in private schools receive much better education than public school students.

15. People living in _____ have on average less education than people living in the other provinces listed.
    a) Ontario
    b) British Columbia
    c) Newfoundland
    d) Alberta

16. Which of the following is *incorrect*?
    a) Those who started, but never finished, post-secondary education have higher unemployment rates than those who started working after high school.
    b) Those with a college diploma have higher unemployment rates than those with a university degree.
    c) Those who started working after high school have higher unemployment rates than those with a college diploma.
    d) Those who started working after high school have higher unemployment rates than those with a university degree.

17. The 1996 census showed that while the average income of Canadian men with a university degree is $60 870, the comparable figure for women is
    a) $13 337.
    b) $23 337.
    c) $33 337.
    d) $43 337.
    e) $53 337.

18. Theodore Sizer showed that bureaucratic schools are often insensitive to the cultural character of the community. He calls this
    a) functional illiteracy.
    b) rigid conformity.
    c) specialization.
    d) inclusiveness.
    e) mainstreaming.

19. Currently, what percentage of people who leave post-secondary schools have not finished their program requirements?
    a) 12
    b) 16
    c) 20
    d) 24
    e) 28

20. *Functional illiteracy* refers to
    a) an inability to read and write at all.
    b) an inability to read at the appropriate level of schooling based on one's age.
    c) an inability to write.
    d) reading and writing skills insufficient for everyday living.

Multiple Choice: Health

1. The *health* of any population is shaped by
    a) the society's cultural patterns.
    b) the society's technology.
    c) the society's social inequality.
    d) all of the above

2. The *World Health organization* reports that _____ people around the world suffer from serious illness due to poverty.
    a) 100 000
    b) 500 000
    c) 750 000
    d) 1 billion
    e) 2.5 billion

3. During the first half of the nineteenth century in Europe and the United States, the improvement in health was primarily due to
    a) the rising standard of living.
    b) medical advances.
    c) changes in cultural values toward medicine.
    d) immigration.

4. In 1900, _____ were the leading causes of deaths in Canada. Today, however, most deaths are caused by
    a) chronic diseases/infectious diseases.
    b) accidents/crime.
    c) infectious diseases/chronic diseases.
    d) cancer/accidents.
    e) crime/accidents.

5. Which of the following were the *leading causes of death* in the U.S. in 1900?
    a) accidents and heart disease
    b) cancer and diphtheria
    c) influenza and pneumonia
    d) lung disease and kidney disease
    e) homicide and diabetes

6. _____ is the study of how health and disease are distributed throughout a society's population.
    a) Demography
    b) Social epidemiology
    c) Epistemology
    d) Medicalization

Society: The Basics, Second Canadian Edition

7. Which of the following is *true* concerning age, sex, and health in Canada?
   a) Across the life course, men are healthier than women.
   b) Males have a slight biological advantage that renders them less likely than females to die before or immediately after birth.
   c) Socialization aids men's health to a greater degree than it does women's health.
   d) Young women are more likely to die than young men.
   e) Across the life course, women are healthier than men.

8. If current trends continue, about 7 of every 100 men will die violently. The corresponding figure for women is
   a) 0.6
   b) 1.6
   c) 3.6
   d) 4.6
   e) 6.6

9. Approximately how many people die from lung cancer each year in Canada?
   a) 500
   b) 4500
   c) 8 500
   d) 12 500
   e) 16 500

10. Which of the following statements is *inaccurate*?
    a) Ninety-five percent of people who suffer from anorexia nervosa and bulimia (eating disorders) are female.
    b) Research shows that young adult women believe that being thin is critical to physical attractiveness.
    c) Research shows that young adult women believe guys like thin girls.
    d) Most men, like women, think that their body shape is not close to what they want it to be.
    e) Our idealized image of beauty leads many young women to diet to the point of risking their health.

11. If untreated, syphilis can lead to
    a) major organ damage.
    b) blindness.
    c) mental disorder.
    d) death.
    e) all of the above

12. About _____ out of every 1 million Canadians have AIDS.
    a) 5
    b) 50
    c) 500
    d) 5000
    e) 50 000

13. North and South America account for _____ percent of all known *HIV infection cases*.
    a) less than 5
    b) 20
    c) 35
    d) 55

14. Male homosexual sexual activity accounts for about _____ percent of transmitted cases of *AIDS* in Canada.
    a) less than 5
    b) 11
    c) 27
    d) 38
    e) 72

15. Assisting in the death of a person suffering from an incurable disease is known as
    a) annihilation.
    b) amniocentesis.
    c) genocide.
    d) euthanasia.

16. The Flexner Report of 1910 resulted in:
    a) expensive medical education.
    b) domination of medical doctors in health care.
    c) closing of schools teaching alternative medicine.
    d) all of the above.

17. *Holistic health* is a reaction to scientific medicine. Which of the following is *not* an emphasis advocates of holistic medicine share?
    a) an emphasis upon the environment in which the person exists
    b) an emphasis upon the responsibility of society for health promotion and care
    c) an emphasis upon optimum health for all
    d) an emphasis upon the home setting for medical treatment

18. _____ refers to a health-care system in which the government owns and operates most medical facilities and employs most physicians.
    a) A health maintenance organization
    b) Socialized health care
    c) A direct-fee system
    d) Holistic medicine

19. The government in the United States pays about ____ percent of medical costs, whereas in Canada, the government pays about ____ percent of medical costs.
    a) 47/70
    b) 50/50
    c) 26/84
    d) 40/60

20. Which country does *not* offer a comprehensive health program to the entire population?
    a) Sweden
    b) Great Britain
    c) the United States
    d) Canada

21. Which of the following *theoretical paradigms* in sociology utilizes concepts like *sick role* and *physician's role* to help explain health behaviour?
    a) social-conflict
    b) social-exchange
    c) symbolic-interaction
    d) structural-functional
    e) cultural materialism

22. Critics fault the _____ *approach* for implying that there are no objective standards of well-being.
    a) symbolic-interactionist
    b) social-conflict
    c) structural-functional
    d) cultural materialist

Matching: Education

1. _____ The percentage of Canadians aged 25 to 64 with a post-secondary diploma or degree.
2. _____ Identified five ways in which large, bureaucratic schools undermine education.
3. _____ Schooling in Canada reflects the value of _____.
4. _____ The percentage of women aged 20 to 29 with post-secondary certificates, diplomas or degrees.
5. _____ The assignment of students to different types of educational programs.
6. _____ The percentage of the elementary and secondary students enrolled in private schools.
7. _____ The amount remaining on student loans in 1997 for those who graduated 2 years earlier (in hundreds of dollars).
8. _____ Suggests that attending post-secondary education is a rite of passage for affluent men and women.
9. _____ Evaluating people on the basis of education degrees.
10. _____ Reading and writing skills inadequate for everyday living.

a. tracking
b. 39
c. equality between the sexes
d. credentialism
e. 51
f. 83
g. social conflict analysis
h. Theodore Sizer
i. functional illiteracy
j. 5.4

Matching: Health
1. ____ The number one cause of death for males in Canada today.
2. ____ The number two cause of death for females in Canada today.
3. ____ The study of how health and disease are distributed throughout a society's population.
4. ____ The percentage of eating disorder victims who are women.
5. ____ The social institution that focuses on combating disease and improving health.
6. ____ An approach to health care that emphasizes prevention of illness and takes account of the person's entire physical and social environment.
7. ____ A medical-care system in which the government owns most facilities and employs most physicians.
8. ____ Percentage of total expenditures on health paid by our governments.
9. ____ The percentage of health expenditures paid by European governments today.
10. ____ Patterns of behaviour defined as appropriate for those who are ill.

a. sick role
b. heart disease
c. socialized medicine
d. 70
e. social epidemiology
f. 80
g. medicine
h. cancer
i. 95
j. holistic medicine

Fill-in-the-blank: Education
1. The social institution through which society provides its members with important knowledge, including basic facts, job skills, and cultural values and norms is termed _____.
2. In Japan, an astonishing _____ *percent* graduate from high school.
3. By _____ all of the states in the U.S. had *mandatory education laws*.
4. Early public schools proclaimed an egalitarian ideology and served to _____ the existing class system.
5. *Functions* served by schooling include: _____, *cultural* _____, *social* _____, *social* _____, and several _____ *functions*.
6. The assignment of students to different types of educational programs is referred to as _____ or _____.

255

7. Although only _____ percent of Canadian elementary and secondary students go to private schools, this percentage is increasing.

8. Research shows that even if schools were exactly the same everywhere, students whose _____ value and encourage education would still perform better.

9. The most crucial factor affecting access to higher education is _____.

10. According to *social-conflict theorists*, schools transform social _____ into personal _____.

11. _____ is evaluating a person on the basis of educational degrees.

12. The average *annual earnings* in 1995 for women with university degrees was $43 337, while women who had not gone on to post-secondary training after graduating from high school earned _____.

13. *Theodore Sizer* identified through his research five ways in which large, _____ schools undermine education, including rigid conformity, numerical rating, rigid expectations, specialization, and little individual responsibility.

14. _____ _____ refers to a lack of reading and writing skills needed for everyday living.

15. An international study of almost 40 nations showed that Canadian grade 8 students scored _____ average on their mathematical abilities.

16. "Teaching the _____: A new Agenda in Gender Equity" showed that _____ outperformed _____ in contemporary Canadian schools.

17. Many instructors argue that computers will _____ replace the teacher in the classroom.

18. Currently, more than _____ percent of those who leave post-secondary schools do so before they finish their program requirement.

Fill-in-the-blank: Health

1. Society shapes the *health* of people in four major ways. These include; cultural patterns define _____, cultural _____ of health change over time, a society's _____ affects people's health, and, social _____ affects people's health.

2. After 1850, *medical advances* began to improve health, primarily by controlling _____ diseases.

3. In 1900, _____ and _____ were leading causes of *death* in Canada.

4. The leading cause of death among men in Canada today is _____.

5. *Social* _____ is the study of how health and disease are distributed throughout a society's population.

6. Death is now rare among young people, with two notable exceptions: a rise in mortality resulting from _____ and, more recently, from _____.

7. _____ _____ tops the list of preventable health hazards.

8. Consumption of *cigarettes* has fallen since 1960, when almost _____ percent of Canadian adults smoked. Today, only about _____ percent of Canadian adults are smokers.

9. _____ percent of people who suffer from *anorexia nervosa* or *bulimia* are women.

10. *HIV* is *infectious* but not _____.

11. Specific behaviours put people at high risk for *HIV* infection. These include _____ sex, sharing _____, and using any kind of _____.

12. _____ is assisting in the death of a person suffering from an incurable disease.

13. _____ *health* is an approach to health care that emphasizes prevention of illness and takes account of the person's entire physical and social environment.

14. The life expectancy of men in Russia is reported to be around 61 years. The life expectance in Finland is about _____.

15. While the U.S. government pays for less than one-half of its people's medical costs, *European* governments pay for about _____ percent of their people's medical costs.

16. Total personal and public expenditures for health care in Canada were _____ percent of GDP in 1999.

17. The _____ _____ refers to patterns of behaviour defined as appropriate for those who are ill.

18. One strength of the _____-_____ *paradigm* lies in revealing that what people view as healthful or harmful depends on numerous factors, many of which are not, strictly speaking, medical.

19. *Social-conflict* analysis focuses attention on the _____ issue, the _____ motive, and medicine as _____ in helping us understand health and medical care in our society.

20. Our authors suggest that we are taking more responsibility for our own health than in times past. Everyone of us, they say, can live better and longer if we avoid _____, _____ sensibly and in moderation, and _____ regularly.

Definition and Short-Answer: Education

1. Describe the four basic *functions* of education as reviewed in the text.
2. What are the major differences between Japan and Canada in the transition between high school and post-secondary schools?
3. What are the five serious problems with the *bureaucratic* nature of our educational system?
4. What are some of the major issues surrounding private schools in Canada?
5. What are the important consequences resulting from acquiring a post-secondary diploma or degree?
6. What is the important criticism of the social-conflict perspective on education?

7. What are the major *problems* in Canadian education? Identify the specific factors involved in each problem identified. What is one recommendation you have to solving each of the problems?
8. What are the important causes and consequences of how we deal with boys and girls in our schools?

Definition and Short-Answer: Health

1. It is pointed out in the text that the *health* of any population is shaped by important characteristics of the society as a whole. What are three general characteristics and an example of each?
2. How have the *causes of death* changed in Canada over the last century?
3. What is *social epidemiology*? Provide two illustrations of patterns found in Canada.
4. What is *HIV*? What is *AIDS*? How is it transmitted?
5. What is meant by the *sick role*?
6. Describe the three basic characteristics of *holistic medicine*.
7. How does the health-care system in Canada differ from those in other capitalist systems?
8. What are *social-conflict* analysts' arguments about the health care system in Canada?
9. What do *symbolic-interactionists* mean by *socially constructing illness* and *socially constructing treatment*?

PART VI: ANSWERS TO STUDY QUESTIONS

True-False: Education

1. F (p. 345)	6. F (p. 344)	11. F (p. 348)	15. T (p. 351)
2. F (p. 344)	7. T (p. 344)	12. T (p. 348)	16. F (p. 353)
3. F (p. 344)	8. F (p. 346)	13. T (p. 350)	17. T (p. 354)
4. F (p. 344)	9. F (p. 347)	14. F (p. 350)	18. T (p. 354)
5. T (p. 344)	10. T (p. 347)		

True-False: Health

1. F (p. 355)	6. T (p. 359)	11. T (p. 361)	16. F (p. 366)
2. F (p. 357)	7. T (p. 360)	12. F (p. 362)	17. F (p. 367)
3. T (p. 358)	8. F (p. 360)	13. F (p. 364)	18. T (p. 368)
4. T (p. 358)	9. T (p. 361)	14. T (p. 366)	19. T (p. 369)
5. T (p. 359)	10. F (p. 361)	15. T (p. 366)	20. T (p. 369)

Multiple Choice: Education

1. a (p. 343)	6. e (p. 344)	11. b (p. 347)	16. a (p. 351)
2. c (p. 344)	7. a (p. 344)	12. c (p. 347)	17. d (p. 351)
3. c (p. 344)	8. c (p. 347)	13. e (p. 348)	18. b (p. 352)
4. d (p. 344)	9. b (pp. 347-348)	14. d (p. 348)	19. c (p. 353)
5. d (p. 344)	10. a (p. 347)	15. c (p. 350)	20. d (p. 354)

Society: The Basics, Second Canadian Edition

Multiple Choice: Health
1. d (pp.355-356)
2. d (p. 356)
3. a (p. 356)
4. c (pp.356-257)
5. c (p. 357)
6. b (p. 357)
7. e (p. 357)
8. d (p. 358)
9. e (p. 358)
10. d (p. 359)
11. d (p. 359)
12. c (p. 360)
13. a (p. 360)
14. d (p. 361)
15. d (p. 361)
16. d (p. 362)
17. b (p. 364)
18. b (p. 365)
19. a (p. 367)
20. d (p. 366)
21. d (p. 367)
22. a (p. 368)

Matching: Education
1. b (p. 344)
2. h (pp.352-353)
3. c (p. 345)
4. e (p. 346)
5. a (p. 348)
6. j (p. 348)
7. f (p. 350)
8. g (p. 351)
9. d (p. 351)
10. i (p. 354)

Matching: Health
1. h (p. 356)
2. b (p. 356)
3. e (p. 357)
4. i (p. 359)
5. g (p. 355)
6. j (p. 364)
7. c (p. 365)
8. d (p. 367)
9. f (p. 367)
10. a (p. 367)

Fill-in-the-blank: Education
1. education (p. 343)
2. 96 (p. 344)
3. 1918 (p. 344)
4. reproduce/perpetuate (p. 346)
5. socialization, innovation, integration, placement, latent (pp. 347)
6. streaming, tracking (p. 348)
7. 5.4 (p. 348)
8. families (p. 350)
9. money (p. 350)
10. privilege, merit (p. 351)
11. Credentialism (p. 351)
12. $25 786 (p. 351)
13. bureaucratic (p. 352)
14. Functional illiteracy (p. 354)
15. slightly above (p. 354)
16. boys, girls, boys (p. 354)
17. never (pp. 355)
18. 20 (p. 353)

Fill-in-the-blank: Health
1. health, standards, technology, inequality (pp. 355-356)
2. infectious (p. 356)
3. influenza, pneumonia (p. 357)
4. cancer (p. 356)
5. epidemiology (p. 357)
6. accidents, AIDS (p. 357)
7. Cigarette smoking (p. 358)
8. 45, 25 (p. 358)
9. 95 (p. 359)

10. contagious (p. 360)
11. anal, needles, drugs (p. 360)
12. Euthanasia (p. 361)
13. Holistic (p. 364)
14. 74 (p. 365)
15. 80 (p. 367)
16. 9.2 (p. 366)
17. sick role (p. 367)
18. symbolic-interaction (pp. 367-368)
19. access, profit, politics (p. 369)
20. tobacco, eat, exercise (p. 369)

PART VII: IN FOCUS—IMPORTANT ISSUES
1. Briefly characterize *schooling* in each of the following countries.
    A. India

    B. United States

    C. Japan

    D. Canada

2. Illustrate each of the following *functions of schooling*.
    A. Socialization

    B. Cultural Innovation

C. Social Integration

D. Social Placement

3. Identify three *latent functions* of schooling.

4. In what ways do social-conflict theorists believe each of the following leads to social inequality in schooling?
   A. Social Control

   B. Standardized Testing

   C. School Tracking

5. What is the evidence that schools have problems in the following areas?
   A. Discipline and Violence

   B. Student Passivity

C. Dropping Out

D. Academic Standards

6. What are three important issues confronting schools over the next generation?

7. What is *health*?

8. What are the five major ways in which society shapes people's *health*?

9. Generally describe the health of people living in *low-income countries*.

10. What was the impact of *industrialization* on health in Canada and Europe?

11. Briefly discuss the health patterns found in Canada using the following variables:
    A. Age and Gender

    B. Social Class, Ethnicity and Race

12. How significant a health problem is the each of the following? Provide demographic evidence of illness and disease for each as discussed in the text.
    A. Cigarette Smoking

    B. Eating Disorders

    C. Sexually Transmitted Diseases

13. According to legal and medical experts, how is *death* defined?

14. Do people have the *right to die*?

15. What are the laws in Canada concerning *euthanasia*? What is your opinion on this issue? Make reference to the two examples mentioned in the text.

16. Describe impact of the rise of *scientific medicine* on health care in the United States.

17. What are the components of *holistic medicine*?

18. What is the role of alternative medicine in the overall health strategy in Canada?

19. Briefly summarize how medical care is paid for in the following *socialist societies*:
    A. the People's Republic of China

    B. the Russian Federation

20. Briefly summarize how medical care is paid for in the following *capitalist societies*.
    A. Sweden

    B. United States

21. How expensive is medical care in Canada? How do we pay for this medical care?

22. According to structural-functionalist analysis, what are the components of the *sick role*?

23. What is the *physician's role*?

24. What do symbolic-interactionists mean by the *social construction of illness*?

25. According to social-conflict analysts, what are the three ways in which health care is related to *social inequality*? Describe and illustrate each of these.

26. Identify and describe the four *trends* identified by the authors concerning health and health care in Canada over the next several decades.

PART VIII: ANALYSIS AND COMMENT

Window on the World–Global Map 14-1
"Illiteracy in Global Perspective"
Key Points: Questions:

Seeing Ourselves–National Map 14-1
"School Attendance, aged 15-24 years, Canada, 1995-1996"
Key Points: Questions:

Social Diversity
"'Cooling Out' the Poor: Transforming Disadvantage into Deficiency"
Key Points: Questions:

Society: The Basics, Second Canadian Edition

Applying Sociology
"Gender and Educational Achievement: Why Are the Boys No Longer at the Top of the Class?"

Key Points: Questions:

Social Diversity
"Masculinity: A Threat to Health?"

Key Points: Questions:

Window on the World—Global Map 14-2
"HIV Infection of Adults in Global Perspective"

Key Points: Questions:

Global Sociology
"When Health Fails: A Report from Russia"

Key Points: Questions:

Controversy and Debate
"The Genetic Crystal Ball: Do We Really Want to Look?"

Key Points: Questions:

Population, Urbanization, and Environment

PART I: CHAPTER OUTLINE

1. Demography: The Study of Population
   A. Fertility
   B. Mortality
   C. Migration
   D. Population Growth
   E. Population Composition
2. History and Theory of Population Growth
   A. Malthusian Theory
   B. Demographic Transition Theory
   C. Global Population Today: A Brief Survey
3. Urbanization: The Growth of Cities
   A. The Evolution of Cities
   B. The Growth of North American Cities
   C. Suburbs and Urban Decline
   D. Megalopolis: Regional Cities
4. Urbanization as a Way of Life
   A. Ferdinand Tönnies: *Gemeinschaft* and *Gesellschaft*
   B. Emile Durkheim: Mechanical and Organic Solidarity
   C. Georg Simmel: The Blasé Urbanite
   D. Robert Park and Louis Wirth: Walking the Streets in Chicago
   E. Urban Ecology
   F. Urban Political Economy
5. Urbanization in Low-Income Countries
6. Environment and Society
   A. The Global Dimension
   B. Technology and the Environmental Deficit
   C. Culture: Growth and Limits
   D. Solid Waste: The Disposable Society
   E. Water and Air
   F. The Rain Forests
   G. Environmental Racism
7. Looking Ahead: Toward a Sustainable World
8. Summary
9. Key Concepts
10. Critical-Thinking Questions
11. Applications and Exercises
12. Sites to See

Society: The Basics, Second Canadian Edition

PART II: LEARNING OBJECTIVES

1. To learn the basic concepts used by demographers to study populations.
2. To be able to compare Malthusian theory and demographic transition theory.
3. To be able to recognize how populations differ in industrial and nonindustrial societies.
4. To gain an understanding of the worldwide urbanization process, and to be able to put it into historical perspective.
5. To be able to describe demographic changes in Canada throughout its history.
6. To consider urbanism as a way of life as viewed by several historical figures in sociology.
7. To consider the idea of urban ecology.
8. To gain an appreciation for the global dimension of the natural environment.
9. To develop an understanding of how sociology can help us confront environmental issues.
10. To be able to discuss the dimensions of the "logic of growth" and the "limits to growth" as issues and realities confronting our world.
11. To be able to identify and discuss major environmental issues confronting our world today.
12. To begin to develop a sense about the ingredients for a sustainable society and world in the century to come.

PART III: KEY CONCEPTS

Population:

age-sex pyramid

crude birth rate

crude death rate

demographic transition theory

demography

fertility

infant mortality rate

life expectancy

migration

mortality

sex ratio

zero population growth

Urbanization:

Census Agglomerations (CAs)

Census Metropolitan Areas (CMAs)

Gemeinschaft

Gesellschaft

megalopolis

metropolis

suburbs

urbanization

Environment:

ecologically sustainable culture

ecology

ecosystem

environmental deficit

environmental racism

greenhouse effect

natural environment

rain forests

urban ecology

PART IV: IMPORTANT RESEARCHERS

Ferdinand Tönnies   Georg Simmel

Robert Park   Donella Meadows

Emile Durkheim   Thomas Malthus

Louis Wirth

PART V: STUDY QUESTIONS

True-False–Population and Urbanization

1. T F Demographers using what is known as the *crude birth rate* only take into account women of childbearing age in the calculation for this figure.
2. T F Canada, using the demographer's *natural growth rate* measure, is experiencing a significant decline in population.
3. T F Population growth in Canada and other high-income nations is well below the world average of 1.4 percent.
4. T F A significantly larger percentage of the Canadian population over the next two decades will be comprised of *childbearing-aged women* than at any other period in our nation's history.
5. T F The world's population reached 1 billion in 1800, 2 billion in 1930, 3 billion in 1962, 4 billion in 1974, 5 billion in 1987, and 6 billion in 1999.
6. T F *Malthusian theory* predicted that while population would increase in a *geometric progression*, food supplies would increase only by an *arithmetic progression*.
7. T F According to *demographic transition theory*, population patterns are linked to a society's level of technological development.
8. T F In low-income countries throughout the world, birth rates have *fallen* since 1950.
9. T F In the mid-eighteenth century, the *Industrial Revolution* triggered a *second urban revolution*.
10. T F Montreal was Canada's largest city at the start of the 20th century.
11. T F Urban decentralization gave rise to the *metropolis*.
12. T F Emile Durkheim termed social bonds based on specialization as *organic solidarity*.
13. T F The *third urban revolution* began during the middle of the twentieth century in low-income societies and continues to this day.

14. T F The *urban political economy model* takes an ecological approach that sees the city as a "natural" organism, with particular districts and neighbourhoods developing according to an internal logic.

True-False-Environment

1. T F The *natural environment* includes the air, water, and soil, but not living organisms.
2. T F The cultural values of material comfort, progress, and science form the foundation for the *logic of growth* thesis.
3. T F The *limits to growth* thesis, stated simply, is that humanity must implement policies to restrain the growth of population, cut back on production, and use fewer natural resources in order to head off environmental collapse.
4. T F The limits to growth theorists are also referred to as *neo-Malthusians*.
5. T F Canada is being characterized in the text as a *disposable society*.
6. T F Over fifty percent of solid waste in Canada is either *burned* or *recycled*.
7. T F Almost one-half of all household trash in Canada is composed of plastic, glass, and food waste.
8. T F According to what scientists call the *hydrological cycle*, the earth naturally recycles water and refreshes the land.
9. T F The global consumption of *water* has tripled since 1950 and is expanding faster than the world's population.
10. T F Households around the world account for more *water use* than does industry.
11. T F *Biodiversity* tends to be relatively low in rain forest environments.
12. T F The *greenhouse effect* is the result of too little carbon dioxide in the atmosphere.

Multiple-Choice-Population and Urbanization

1. The incidence of childbearing in a country's population refers to
    a) fertility.
    b) fecundity.
    c) demography.
    d) sex ratio.
    e) life expectancy.

2. *Fecundity*, or maximum possible childbearing, is sharply reduced in practice by
    a) cultural norms.
    b) finances.
    c) personal choice.
    d) all of the above

3. The movement of people into and out of a specified territory is
    a) demographic transition.
    b) migration.
    c) fecundity.
    d) mortality.
    e) fertility.

4. Which region of the world has both at once the *highest* birth rate, death rate, and infant mortality rate?
   a) Latin America
   b) Asia
   c) Europe
   d) Oceania
   e) Africa

5. The *sex ratio* in Canada is
   a) 85.
   b) 100.
   c) 90.
   d) 105.
   e) 98.

6. How many people are added to the planet *each year*?
   a) 18 million
   b) 27 million
   c) 52 million
   d) 80 million

7. In 1999, the world population stood at approximately
   a) 2 billion.
   b) 4 billion.
   c) 6 billion.
   d) 8 billion.

8. During the twentieth century, the world's population increased _____-fold.
   a) two
   b) three
   c) four
   d) five
   e) six

9. *Demographic transition theory* links population patterns to a society's
   a) religious beliefs and practices.
   b) technological development.
   c) natural resources.
   d) sexual norms.

10. *Stage 3* of the demographic transition theory is characterized by
    a) increasing death rates.
    b) increasing birth rates.
    c) decreasing death rates.
    d) none of the above

11. The *first city* ever to have existed is argued to be
    a) Athens.
    b) Cairo.
    c) Tikal.
    d) Jericho.
    e) Rome

Study Guide

12. According to the text, the *second urban revolution* was triggered by
    a) the fall of Rome.
    b) the post-World War II baby boom.
    c) the Industrial Revolution.
    d) the discovery of the New World.
    e) the fall of Greece.

13. The period called *the metropolitan era* occurred between
    a) 1624-1800.
    b) 1860-1950.
    c) 1950-1970.
    d) 1970 to the present.

14. The period of *1950 to the present* is described in the text as
    a) urban decentralization.
    b) the metropolitan era.
    c) urban expansion.
    d) the second urban revolution.

15. A vast urban region containing a number of cities and their surrounding suburbs is known as a
    a) metropolis.
    b) suburb.
    c) Gemeinschaft.
    d) megalopolis.

16. *Ferdinand Tönnies'* concept referring to the type of social organization by which people stand apart based on self-interest is
    a) megalopolis.
    b) sector model.
    c) *Gesellschaft*.
    d) multi-nuclei model.
    e) *Gemeinschaft*.

17. Emile Durkheim described traditional, rural life as _____, social bonds based on common sentiments and shared moral values.
    a) organic solidarity
    b) mechanical solidarity
    c) *Gesellschaft*
    d) edge cities

18. Robert Park, of the *Chicago school*, saw the city as
    a) a living organism—a human kaleidoscope.
    b) a crush of humanity.
    c) devoid of the human spirit.
    d) villages of chaos and destruction.

19. The link between the *physical* and *social* dimensions of cities is known as
    a) Gesellschaft.
    b) urban ecology.
    c) organic solidarity.
    d) mechanical solidarity.
    e) demography.

20. _____ *analysis* is a branch of urban ecology that investigates what people in particular neighbourhoods have in common.
    a) Wedge-shaped
    b) Concentric zones
    c) Multicentered model
    d) Social area

21. This model of urbanization claims that city life is defined by people with power, and that capitalism turns cities into real estate to be traded for profit.
    a) concentric zone
    b) ecological
    c) urban political economy
    d) urban renewal strategy

22. It is predicted that this percentage of people in low-income countries will live in *urban areas* by 2005.
    a) 82
    b) 25
    c) 50
    d) 67
    e) 42

Multiple Choice – Environment

1. _____ is the study of the interaction of living organisms and the natural environment.
    a) Environmentalism
    b) Sociobiology
    c) Ecosystem
    d) Ecology

2. The Greek meaning of the word *eco* is
    a) weather.
    b) satisfaction.
    c) house.
    d) work.
    e) material.

3. A(n) _____ is a system composed of the interaction of all living organisms and their natural environment.
    a) ecosystem
    b) environment
    c) biosphere
    d) ecology

4. People in high-income nations represent fifteen percent of the world's population, but consume ____ percent of the world's *energy*.
    a) twenty-five
    b) fifty
    c) sixty-five
    d) eighty
    e) ninety-eight

5. Which of the following cultural values form the foundation of the *logic of growth* perspective?
   a) material comfort
   b) progress
   c) science
   d) all of the above
   e) none of the above

6. Which of the following is *not* a projection for the next century using the *limits of growth thesis*?
   a) stabilizing, then declining population
   b) declining industrial output per capita
   c) declining resources
   d) increasing, then declining pollution
   e) increasing food per capita

7. How many kilograms of *solid waste* is thrown out by each of us daily?
   a) 0.8
   b) 1.8
   c) 2.8
   d) 3.8
   e) 4.8

8. Which type of solid waste represents about *one-half* of all household trash in Canada?
   a) metal products
   b) yard waste
   c) paper
   d) plastic
   e) glass

9. What percentage of the solid waste in the Canada ends up in a landfill?
   a) 90
   b) 80
   c) 70
   d) 60
   e) 15

10. While industry accounts for 25 percent of water usage globally, individuals account for _____ percent of usage.
    a) 90
    b) 65
    c) 50
    d) 25
    e) 10

11. *Rain forests* cover approximately _____ percent of the earth's land surface.
    a) 1
    b) 7
    c) 2
    d) 11

12. Rain forests are home to almost _____ percent of our planet's species.
    a) 90
    b) 75
    c) 50
    d) 30
    e) 10

13. A way of life that meets the needs of the present generation without threatening the environmental legacy of future generations refers to
    a) ecologically sustainable culture.
    b) the Green Revolution.
    c) environmental racism.
    d) the greenhouse effect

14. Strategies recommended for creating a sustainable ecosystem include
    a) conservation of finite resources.
    b) bringing population under control.
    c) reducing waste.
    d) all of the above

Matching–Population and Urbanization

1. _____ The incidence of childbearing in a country's population.
2. _____ Maximum possible childbearing.
3. _____ A theory claiming that population would soon rise out of control.
4. _____ A thesis linking population patterns to a society's level of technological development.
5. _____ The concentration of humanity into cities.
6. _____ 1860-1950.
7. _____ Developed the concepts *Gemeinschaft* and *Gesellschaft*.
8. _____ Developed the concepts of mechanical and organic solidarity.
9. _____ A type of social organization by which people stand apart from one another in pursuit of self-interest.
10. _____ Social bonds based on common sentiments and shared moral values.
11. _____ Argued that urbanites develop a blasé attitude, selectively tuning out much of what goes on around them.
12. _____ Saw the city as a living organism, truly a human kaleidoscope.

a. Ferdinand Tönnies
b. mechanical solidarity
c. fertility
d. *Gesellschaft*
e. demographic transition theory
f. metropolitan era
g. Robert Parks
h. Malthusian theory
i. Emile Durkheim
j. fecundity
k. urbanization
l. Georg Simmel

Matching—Environment

1. _____ The earth's surface and atmosphere, including living organisms as well as the air, soil, and other resources necessary to sustain life.
2. _____ The study of the interaction of living organisms and the natural environment.
3. _____ The system composed of the interaction of all living organisms and their natural environment.
4. _____ Profound and negative long-term harm to the natural environment caused by humanity's focus on short-term material affluence.
5. _____ The number of litres of water consumed by a person in Canada over a lifetime (in millions).
6. _____ Regions of dense forestation most of which circle the globe close to the equator.
7. _____ A rise in the earth's average temperature due to an increasing concentration of carbon dioxide in the atmosphere.
8. _____ The pattern by which environmental hazards are greatest in proximity to poor people and especially minorities.
9. _____ The number of people added to the world's population each year (net gain in millions).
10. _____ The percentage of Canadians who, at the end of the 1990s, listed "environment" as one of the top three pressing issues that our leaders should deal with.

a. natural environment
b. greenhouse effect
c. 45
d. less than 10
e. 80
f. ecology
g. environmental deficit
h. rain forests
i. environmental racism
j. ecosystem

Fill-in-the-blank—Population and Urbanization

1. _____ refers to the study of human population.

2. _____ is the incidence of childbearing in a country's population.

3. _____ refers to the incidence of death in a country's population.

4. On January 1, 2000, there were about 30.6 million people living in Canada. Between July 1, 1999 and July 1, 2000, there were 334 000 births in Canada. That yields a *crude birth rate* of _____.

5. Movement out of a country—or _____—is measured in terms of an _____ rate.

Society: The Basics, Second Canadian Edition

6. The _____ _____ refers to the number of males for every hundred females in a given population.

7. *Thomas Malthus* saw population increasing according to _____ progression, and food production increasing in _____ progression.

8. _____ _____ *theory* is the thesis that population patterns are linked to a society's level of technological development.

9. _____ _____ _____ refers to the level of reproduction that maintains population at a steady state.

10. The term _____ is from the Greek meaning "mother city."

11. _____ refers to the concentration of humanity into cities.

12. Statistics Canada recognizes 25 cities and surrounding areas where more than 100 000 live in the urban core. These are called CMAs or _____ _____ _____.

13. Toronto is the largest CMA with 4.7 million people. The smallest is _____ _____ with about 127 000.

14. _____ refers to a type of social organization by which people are bound closely together by kinship and tradition.

15. _____ _____ is the study of the link between the physical and social dimensions of cities.

16. In 1950, only seven cities in the world had populations over five million, and only two of these were in low-income countries. By 1999, _____ cities has passed this mark, and _____ were in low-income countries.

Fill-in-the-blank—Environment

1. The _____ _____ refers to the earth's surface and atmosphere, including living organisms, air, water, soil, and other resources necessary to sustain life.

Study Guide

2. An _____ is defined as the system composed of the interaction of all living organisms and their natural environment.

3. The concept of *environmental deficit* implies three important ideas. First, the state of the environment is a _____ _____. Second, much environmental damage is _____. And third, in some respects environmental damage is _____.

4. Core values that underlie cultural patterns in Canada include progress, material comfort, and science. Such values form the foundation for the _____ *thesis*.

5. The _____ *thesis* states that humanity must implement policies to control the growth of population, material production, and the use of resources in order to avoid environmental collapse.

6. It is estimated that fifty percent of household trash is _____.

7. In Canada about _____ percent of *solid waste* ends up in landfills.

8. The earth naturally recycles water and refreshes the land through what scientists call the _____ *cycle*.

9. We need to curb *water consumption* by industry, which uses _____ percent of the global total, and by farming, which consumes _____ of the total for irrigation.

10. Strategies for creating an *ecologically sustainable culture* include bringing _____ _____ under control, _____ finite resources, and reducing _____.

Definition and Short-Answer–Population and Urbanization

1. What are the three basic factors which determine the *size* and *growth rate* of a population? Define each of these concepts.
2. Differentiate between *Malthusian theory* and *demographic transition theory* as perspectives on population growth.
3. What are the four stages in the *demographic transition theory*? Describe each.
4. Identify and describe the five *periods of growth* of Canadian cities.
5. Differentiate between the concepts *metropolis* and *megalopolis*.
6. Differentiate between the perspectives of *Louis Wirth* and *Robert Park* concerning urbanization.

7. Describe how *urbanization* patterns are changing around the world.
8. Compare the views of *Ferdinand Tönnies* and *Emile Durkheim* concerning urbanization.
9. What is *urban ecology*? What are two criticisms of this approach?
10. Discuss significant points made in the text about the *low-growth north* and the *high-growth south*.
11. What is the perspective offered by *Georg Simmel* on urbanism?
12. What are the three *urban revolutions*? Briefly describe each.

Definition and Short-Answer—Environment

1. Differentiate between the concepts *ecology* and *natural environment*.
2. What three important ideas are implied by the concept *environmental deficit*?
3. Briefly describe the pattern of word *population growth* prior to and after the Industrial Revolution.
4. Critically differentiate between the *logic of growth* and the *limits to growth* views concerning the relationship between human technology and the natural environment.
5. What is meant by the term *disposable society*? What evidence is being presented to support this view of Canada?
6. Review the global research concerning either *water pollution* or *air pollution*.
7. Discuss the connection between the depletion of the rain forest and global warming and declining biodiversity.
8. What is the *biodiversity crisis* and why is it so significant?

PART VI: ANSWERS TO STUDY QUESTIONS

True-False—Population and Urbanization

1. F (p. 376)	5. T (p. 380)	9. T (p. 385)	12. T (p. 388)
2. F (p. 377)	6. T (p. 381)	10. T (p. 386)	13. T (p. 390)
3. T (p. 377)	7. T (p. 381)	11. F (p. 386)	14. F (pp. 389-390)
4. F (p. 380)	8. T (p. 382)		

True-False—Environment

1. F (p. 390)	4. T (p. 393)	7. F (p. 393)	10. F (p. 395)
2. T (p. 392)	5. T (p. 393)	8. T (pp. 394-395)	11. F (p. 398)
3. T (p. 393)	6. F (p. 394)	9. T (p. 395)	12. F (p. 398)

Multiple-Choice—Population and Urbanization

1. a (p. 376)	7. c (p. 380)	13. b (p. 386)	18. a (p. 388)
2. d (p. 376)	8. c (p. 380)	14. a (p. 386)	19. b (p. 389)
3. b (p. 377)	9. b (p. 381)	15. d (p. 386)	20. d (p. 389)
4. e (p. 376)	10. c (p. 382)	16. c (p. 388)	21. c (p. 390)
5. e (p. 378)	11. d (p. 384)	17. b (p. 388)	22. c (p. 390)
6. d (p. 380)	12. c (p. 385)		

Multiple-Choice–Environment

1. d (p. 390)
2. c (p. 391)
3. a (p. 391)
4. d (p. 392)
5. d (p. 392)
6. e (p. 393)
7. b (p. 393)
8. c (p. 393)
9. b (p. 394)
10. e (p. 395)
11. b (p. 398)
12. c (p. 398)
13. a (p. 400)
14. d (p. 400)

Matching–Population and Urbanization

1. c (p. 376)
2. j (p. 376)
3. h (p. 380)
4. e (p. 381)
5. k (p. 383)
6. f (p. 386)
7. a (p. 387)
8. i (p. 388)
9. d (p. 388)
10. b (p. 388)
11. l (p. 388)
12. g (p. 388)

Matching–Environment

1. a (p. 390)
2. f (p. 390)
3. j (p. 391)
4. g (p. 392)
5. c (p. 395)
6. h (p. 398)
7. b (p. 398)
8. i (p. 399)
9. e (p. 399)
10. d (p. 401)

Fill-in-the-blank–Population and Urbanization

1. Demography (p. 376)
2. Fertility (p. 376)
3. Mortality (p. 376)
4. 10.9 (p. 376)
5. emigration, emigration (p. 377)
6. sex ratio (p. 378)
7. geometric, arithmetic (p. 381)
8. Demographic transition (p. 381)
9. Zero population growth (p. 382)
10. metropolis (p. 386)
11. Urbanization (p. 383)
12. Census Metropolitan Areas (p. 387)
13. Thunder Bay (p. 387)
14. *Gemeinschaft* (p. 388)
15. Urban ecology (p. 389)
16. 37, 26 (p. 390)

Fill-in-the-blank–Environment

1. natural environment (p. 390)
2. ecosystem (p. 391)
3. social issue, unintended, reversible (p. 392)
4. logic of growth (p. 392)
5. limits to growth (p. 393)
6. paper (p. 393)
7. 80 (p. 394)
8. hydrological (p. 394)
9. 20, two-thirds (p. 395)
10. population growth, conserving, waste (p. 400)

Society: The Basics, Second Canadian Edition

PART VII: IN FOCUS – IMPORTANT ISSUES
1. How is each of the following concepts defined? How does each of the following factors affect *population size*?
    A. fertility

    B. crude birth rate

    C. fecundity

    D. mortality

    E. crude death rate

    F. life expectancy

    G. migration

    H. immigration

I. emigration

2. What is the *natural growth rate* of Canada? How does it compare to the natural growth rate in other parts of the world like Asia and Africa? Explain.

3. In what ways is the *age-sex pyramid* an important measure of population growth?

4. Briefly describe the components of each of the following theories of population growth.
    A. Malthusian theory

    B. Demographic Transition Theory

5. What is meant by the *low-growth North*?

6. What is meant by the *high-growth South*?

7. Identify and describe the three *urban revolutions*.
   A. First

   B. Second

   C. Third

8. Describe each of the following periods in the *growth of cities* in Canada.
   A. Colonial Settlement

   B. Urban Expansion

   C. the Metropolitan Era

   D. Urban Decentralization

9. How did each of the following theorists characterize cities and the process of *urbanization*?
   A. Ferdinand Tönnies

B. Emile Durkheim

C. Georg Simmel

D. Robert Park

E. Louis Wirth

10. What is *urban ecology*?

11. How is the *urban political economy model* different from the ecological model in term of understanding urban issues?

12. Differentiate between each of the following views concerning environmental issues:
    A. the Logic of Growth

    B. the Limits to Growth

Society: The Basics, Second Canadian Edition

13. What are two important points being made in the text concerning each of the following?
    A. Solid Waste

    B. Water

    C. Air

14. Why are the *rain forests* so important to the world and all living things?

15. What are the three recommendations being made for establishing an *ecologically sustainable culture*?

16. What specific ideas would you recommend implementing to encourage each of these?

Study Guide

PART VIII: ANALYSIS AND COMMENT

Seeing Ourselves–National Map 15-1
"Population Movement, Canada 1991-1996"

Key Points: Questions:

Window on the World–Global Map 15-1
"Population Growth in Global Perspective"

Key Points: Questions:

Global Sociology
"Empowering Women: The Key to Controlling Population Growth"

Key Points: Questions:

Critical Thinking
"Why Grandmother Had No Trash"

Key Points: Questions:

Window on the World–Global Map 15-2
"Water Consumption in Global Perspective"
Key Points: Questions:

Seeing Ourselves–National Map 15-1
"Percentage of People Travelling to Work by Car, Truck, Van, or Motorcycle, Canada, 1996"
Key Points: Questions:

Controversy and Debate
"Reclaiming the Environment: What Are You Willing to Give Up?"
Key Points: Questions:

Study Guide

Social Change: Modern and Postmodern Societies

PART I: CHAPTER OUTLINE
1. What is Social Change?
2. Causes of Social Change
    A. Culture and Change
    B. Conflict and Change
    C. Ideas and Change
    D. Demographic Change
    E. Social Movements and Change
3. Modernity
    A. Ferdinand Tönnies: The Loss of Community
    B. Emile Durkheim: The Division of Labour
    C. Max Weber: Rationalization
    D. Karl Marx: Capitalism
4. Structural-Functional Analysis: The Theory of Mass Society
    A. The Mass Scale of Modern Life
    B. The Ever-Expanding State
5. Social Conflict Analysis: The Theory of Class Society
    A. Capitalism
    B. Persistent Inequality
6. Modernity and the Individual
    A. Mass Society: Problems of Identity
    B. Class Society: Problems of Powerlessness
7. Modernity and Progress
    A. Modernity and Global Variation
8. Postmodernity
9. Looking Ahead: Modernization and Our Global Future
10. Summary
11. Key Concepts
12. Critical-Thinking Questions
13. Applications and Exercises
14. Sites to See

PART II: LEARNING OBJECTIVES

1. To be able to identify and describe the four general characteristics of social change.
2. To be able to identify and illustrate the different sources of social change.
3. To be able to discuss the perspectives on social change as offered by Ferdinand Tönnies, Emile Durkheim, Max Weber, and Karl Marx.
4. To be able to identify and describe the general characteristics of modernization.
5. To be able to identify the key ideas of two major interpretations of modern society: mass society and class society.
6. To be able to discuss the ideas of postmodernist thinkers and critically consider their relevance for our society.

PART III: KEY CONCEPTS

anomie

class society

division of labour

mass society

modernity

modernization

other-directedness

postmodernity

relative deprivation

social change

social character

social movement

tradition-directedness

PART IV: IMPORTANT RESEARCHERS

Karl Marx   Emile Durkheim

William Ogburn

Ferdinand Tönnies

Herbert Marcuse

David Riesman

Max Weber

PART V: STUDY QUESTIONS

True-False

1. T F *Cultural lag* refers to the fact that some cultures are more technologically advanced, and therefore superior to, some other cultures.
2. T F Three pivotal *sources* of social change are *diffusion, invention,* and *discovery*.
3. T F As a source of social change, *diffusion* involves the movement of cultural traits from one society to another.
4. T F *Max Weber* argued that technology and conflict are more important than ideas in transforming society.
5. T F Alcoholics Anonymous is an example of a *redemptive social movement* as it seeks radical change in some individuals.
6. T F One in ten Canadians is over age 65.
7. T F *Mass-society theory* argues that social movements attract socially isolated people who seek, through their membership, a sense of identity and purpose.
8. T F *Modernity* is defined as social patterns resulting from industrialization.
9. T F According to *Peter Berger*, a characteristic of modernization is the decline of personal choice.
10. T F The concepts of *Gemeinschaft* and *Gesellschaft* were developed by *Ferdinand Tönnies* and pertain to his theory of modernization.
11. T F Emile Durkheim suggested that modern society is characterized by *mechanical solidarity*.

12. T F According to our authors, *Emile Durkheim's* view of modernity is both more complex and more positive than that of *Ferdinand Tönnies*.

13. T F Compared to *Emile Durkheim, Max Weber* was more critical of modern society, believing that the rationalization of bureaucracies would cause people to become alienated.

14. T F Karl Marx focussed much attention on *bureaucracy* as a means through which socialist societies could overcome the alienating qualities of capitalism.

15. T F A *mass society* is one in which industry and bureaucracy have enhanced social ties.

16. T F *Class society theory* maintains that persistent social inequality undermines modern society's promise of individual freedom.

17. T F A basic criticism of *class-society* theory is that it overlooks the increasing prosperity of modern societies.

18. T F According to *David Riesman*, a type of social character he labels *other-directedness* is valued in rapidly changing industrial societies.

19. T F People in Canada are less likely than people in many other industrialized societies to see *scientific advances* as helping humankind.

20. T F Herbert Marcuse argues that technological advances in modern society have increased people's control over their own lives.

21. T F *Postmodernity* refers to the recent trend in industrialized societies of a return to traditional values and practices.

22. T F The *communitarianism movement* rests on the simple premise that "strong rights presume strong responsibilities."

Multiple Choice

1. The transformation of culture and social institutions over time refers to
   a) social statics.
   b) social change.
   c) cultural lag.
   d) modernity.

2. *William Ogburn's* theory of _____ states that material culture changes faster than nonmaterial culture.
   a) modernity
   b) cultural lag
   c) modernization
   d) anomie
   e) rationalization

3. _____ creates change as products, people, and information spread from one society to another.
   a) Invention
   b) Innovation
   c) Alienation
   d) Diffusion
   e) Cultural lag

4. Which of the following types of *social movements* is least threatening to the status quo because it seeks only limited change in only a small part of the population of a society?
   a) redemptive
   b) revolutionary
   c) reformative
   d) residual
   e) alternative

5. _____ is the process of social change begun by industrialization.
   a) Postmodernity
   b) Anomie
   c) Mass society
   d) Modernization
   e) Modernity

6. Who developed the theory of *Gemeinschaft* and *Gesellschaft*, arguing that the Industrial Revolution weakened the social fabric of family and tradition by introducing a business-like emphasis on facts, efficiency, and money?
   a) Karl Marx
   b) Emile Durkheim
   c) Max Weber
   d) Ferdinand Tönnies

7. For *Emile Durkheim*, modernization is defined by the increasing _____ of a society.
   a) mechanical solidarity
   b) alienation
   c) division of labour
   d) conspicuous consumption

8. In contrast to Ferdinand Tönnies who saw industrialization as amounting to a loss of solidarity, _____ viewed modernization not as a loss of community but as a change from community based on bonds of likeness to community based on economic interdependence.
   a) Emile Durkheim
   b) Karl Marx
   c) Max Weber
   d) Peter Berger

9. For *Max Weber*, modernity means replacing a traditional world view with a(n) _____ way of thinking.
   a) alienated
   b) marginal
   c) mechanical
   d) organic
   e) rational

10. *Karl Marx's* theory underestimated the dominance of _____ in modern society.
    a) inequality
    b) alienation
    c) power
    d) bureaucracy
    e) false consciousness

11. Which of the following is most *accurate*?
    a) Emile Durkheim's concept of organic solidarity refers to social bonds of mutual dependency based on specialization.
    b) Ferdinand Tönnies saw societies as changing from the social organization based on *Gesellschaft* to the social organization based on *Gemeinschaft*.
    c) Peter Berger argued that modern society offers less autonomy than is found in pre-industrial societies.
    d) Emile Durkheim's concept of mechanical solidarity is very similar in meaning to Ferdinand Tönnies' concept of *Gesellschaft*.

12. *Emile Durkheim's* concepts of *mechanical solidarity* and *organic solidarity* are somewhat similar in meaning to the concepts
    a) mass society and class society.
    b) tradition-directedness and other-directedness.
    c) anomie and progress.
    d) *Gemeinschaft* and *Gesellschaft*.
    e) none of the above

13. _____ *theory* focuses on the expanding scale of social life and the rise of the state in the study of modernization.
    a) Dependency
    b) Modernization
    c) Social class
    d) Rationalization
    e) Mass-society

14. _____ *theory* views the process of modernization as being linked to the rise of capitalism, and sees its effects as involving the persistence of social inequality.
    a) Mass-society
    b) Class-society
    c) Modernity
    d) Cultural lag

15. Which social scientist described *modernization* in terms of its effects on *social character*?
    a) Peter Berger
    b) William Ogburn
    c) David Riesman
    d) Herbert Marcuse
    e) David Klein

16. _____ refers to personality patterns common to members of a particular society.
    a) Mass-society
    b) Class-society
    c) Traditionalism
    d) Social character
    e) Autonomy

17. David Riesman suggests that _____ is representative of modern societies.
    a) other-directedness
    b) self-directedness
    c) mechanical-directedness
    d) anomic-directedness

18. _____ *theory* argues that persistent social inequality undermines modern society's promise of individual freedom.
    a) Mass-society
    b) Modernization
    c) Traditional-rational
    d) Mechanical
    e) Class-society

19. _____ suggested that we be critical of *Max Weber's* view that modern society is rational because technological advances rarely empower people; instead, we should focus on the issue of how technology tends to reduce people's control over their own lives.
    a) Emile Durkheim
    b) Herbert Spencer
    c) David Riesman
    d) Herbert Marcuse
    e) Ferdinand Tönnies

20. The *Kaiapo*
    a) is a small society in Brazil.
    b) is a ritual among the Mbuti of the Ituri forest.
    c) is a sacred tradition involving animal sacrifices which has been made illegal by the United States government.
    d) are a people of Asia who represent the *Gesellschaft* concept developed by Ferdinand Tönnies.
    e) is a ritualistic war pattern of the Maring, a New Guinea culture of horticulturalists.

21. According to public opinion polls, in which of the following modern societies does the largest percentage of the population believe that *scientific advances* are helping society?
    a) Great Britain
    b) Japan
    c) the United States
    d) Canada

22. The bright light of "progress" is fading; science no longer holds the answers; cultural debates are intensifying; in important respects, modernity has failed; and social institutions are changing–are all themes running through _____.
   a) class society.
   b) postmodern thinking.
   c) mass society.
   d) social movements.

Matching

1. ____ The transformation of culture and social institutions over time.
2. ____ Social patterns resulting from industrialization.
3. ____ Developed the concepts of *Gemeinschaft* and *Gesellschaft*.
4. ____ Developed the concepts of mechanical and organic solidarity.
5. ____ Argued that modern society was dominated by rationality.
6. ____ Understood modern society as being synonymous with capitalism.
7. ____ A society in which industry and bureaucracy have eroded traditional social ties.
8. ____ A capitalist society with pronounced social stratification.
9. ____ Personality patterns common to members of a particular society.
10. ____ The premise that strong rights presume strong responsibilities.

a. mass society
b. social change
c. Max Weber
d. Ferdinand Tönnies
e. modernity
f. social character
g. Emile Durkheim
h. communitarian
i. class society
j. Karl Marx

Fill-in-the-blank

1. _____ _____ refers to the transformation of culture and social institutions over time.

2. The process of *social change* has four major characteristics, including: social change happens _____ the time, social change is sometimes _____ but often _____, social change is _____, and some changes matter more than _____.

3. As suggested in the text, focussing on culture as a source, *social change* results from three basic processes: _____, _____, and _____.

4. _____ *social movements* aim for limited change, but target everyone.

5. _____-_____ *theory* is a theoretical scheme that links success of any social movement to available resources—including money, human labour, and access to the mass media.

6. _____ refers to social patterns linked to industrialization.

7. According to Peter Berger, four major characteristics of *modernization* include: The decline of small, _____ communities, the _____ of personal choice, increasing social _____, and future orientation and growing awareness of _____.

8. *Emile Durkheim's* concept of *organic solidarity* is closely related to *Ferdinand Tönnies'* concept of _____.

9. _____ is a condition in which society provides little moral guidance to individuals.

10. For *Max Weber*, modernity amounts to the progressive replacement of a traditional world-view with a _____ way of thinking.

11. *Mass society theory* draws upon the ideas of _____, _____, and _____.

12. A _____ *society* is a society in which industry and expanding bureaucracy have eroded traditional social ties.

13. A _____ *society* is a capitalist society with pronounced social stratification.

14. _____ _____ refers to personality patterns common to members of a particular society.

15. *David Riesman* argues that pre-industrial societies promote _____-directedness, or rigid personalities based on conformity to time-honoured ways of living.

16. Five themes have emerged as part of *postmodern thinking*. These include that in important respects, _____ has failed; the bright promise of "_____" is fading; _____ no longer holds the answers; cultural debates are _____; and, social institutions are _____.

Definition and Short-Answer

1. What are four characteristics of *social change*?
2. Five general domains which are involved in *causing* social change are identified and discussed in the text. List these and provide an example for each.
3. Differentiate between perspectives on modernization as offered by *Ferdinand Tönnies, Emile Durkheim, Max Weber,* and *Karl Marx*.
4. What factors of *modernization* do theorists operating from the *mass society* theory focus upon?
5. What are the two types of *social character* identified by *David Riesman*? Define each of these.
6. What are the arguments being made by *postmodernists* concerning social change in modern society? What do critics of this view say?
7. Referring to *Table 16-1*, select a low-income society and compare it to Canada on four elements of society identified in the table. Provide a specific illustration representing a relative comparison for each element.
8. The authors discuss four general types of *social movements*. Identify, define, and illustrate each.
9. Four explanations of *social movements* are discussed in the text. Identify and describe each of these.
10. *Peter Berger* has identified four major characteristics of modernization. What are these? Provide an illustration for each of these.
11. What is your interpretation of the data presented in the *Applying Sociology* box presented at the end of this chapter?

PART VI: ANSWERS TO STUDY QUESTIONS

True-False

1. F (p. 408)	7. T (p. 411)	13. T (p. 415)	18. T (p. 420)
2. T (p. 409)	8. T (p. 412)	14. F (pp.415-416)	19. F (p. 423)
3. T (p. 409)	9. F (p. 413)	15. F (p. 416)	20. F (p. 421)
4. F (p. 410)	10. T (p. 413)	16. T (p. 421)	21. F (p. 423)
5. T (p. 411)	11. F (p. 414)	17. T (p. 419)	22. T (p. 426)
6. T (p. 411)	12. T (p. 414)		

Multiple Choice

1. b (p. 408)	4. e (p. 411)	7. c (p. 414)	10. d (p. 416)
2. b (p. 408)	5. d (p. 412)	8. a (p. 414)	11. a (pp.412-414)
3. d (p. 409)	6. d (p. 413)	9. e (p. 415)	12. d (p. 414)

13. e (p. 416)	16. d (p. 419)	19. d (p. 421)	21. c (p. 423)
14. b (pp. 418-419)	17. a (p. 420)	20. a (p. 422)	22. b (p. 423)
15. c (p. 419)	18. e (p. 421)		

Matching

1. b (p. 408)	4. g (p. 414)	7. a (p. 416)	9. f (p. 419)
2. e (p. 412)	5. c (p. 415)	8. i (p. 418)	10. h (p. 426)
3. d (p. 413)	6. j (p. 415)		

Fill-in-the-blank
1. Social change (p. 408)
2. all, intentional, unplanned, controversial, others (pp. 408-409)
3. invention, discovery, diffusion (p. 409)
4. Reformative (p. 411)
5. Resource-mobilization (p. 411-412)
6. Modernity (p. 412)
7. traditional, expansion, diversity, time (pp. 412-413)
8. *Gesellschaft* (p. 414)
9. Anomie (p. 414)
10. rational (p. 415)
11. Tönnies, Durkheim, Weber (p. 416)
12. mass (p. 416)
13. class (p. 418)
14. Social character (p. 419)
15. tradition (pp. 419-420)
16. modernity, progress, science, intensifying, changing (p. 423)

PART VII: IN FOCUS—IMPORTANT ISSUES

1. What is social change?

2. What are the four major characteristics of the process of *social change*?

3. Provide an illustration for each of the following *causes of social change*.
    A. Culture and Change

B. Invention

C. Discovery

D. Diffusion

E. Conflict and Change

F. Ideas and Change

G. Demographic Change

4. What is modernity?

5. What are the four major characteristics of *modernization*?

6. Briefly summarize the view of modernity as expressed by each of the following theorists.
    A. Ferdinand Tönnies

    B. Emile Durkheim

    C. Max Weber

    D. Karl Marx

7. According to structural-functionalists, what are the essential characteristics of *mass-society*?

8. What is the major problem associated with mass-society? Illustrate:

9. According to conflict theorists, what are the essential characteristics of *class-society*?

10. What is the major problem associated with class-society? Illustrate.

11. What are the five themes shared by *postmodern* thinkers? Provide evidence for two of these themes.

PART VIII: ANALYSIS AND COMMENT

Seeing Ourselves—National Map 16-1
"Population Change, Canada, 1991-1996"

Key Points: Questions:

Global Sociology
"Does 'Modern' Mean 'Progress'? The Case of Brazil's Kaiapo"
Key Points: Questions:

Critical Thinking
"Tracking Change: Is Life in the United States Getting Better or Worse?"
Key Points: Questions:

Controversy and Debate
"Personal Freedom and Social Responsibility: Can We Have It Both Ways?"
Key Points: Questions: